Cesar Chavez

with profiles of
Terence V. Powderly
and Dolores Huerta

World Book, Inc.
a Scott Fetzer company
Chicago

BIOGRAPHICAL ⊕ CONNECTIONS

Writer: E. L. Thompson.

World Book, Inc.
233 N. Michigan Ave.
Chicago, IL 60601

For information about other World Book publications, visit our Web site at **www.worldbook.com** or call **1-800-WORLDBK (967-5325)**.
For information about sales to schools and libraries, call **1-800-975-3250 (United States)**, or **1-800-837-5365 (Canada)**.

Library of Congress Cataloging-in-Publication Data

Thompson, E. L., 1953-
  Cesar Chavez, with profiles of Terence V. Powderly and Dolores Huerta /[writer, E.L. Thompson].
     p. cm. -- (Biographical connections)
  Summary: "A biography of Cesar Chavez, a social activist, union organizer, and spokesperson for the poor. Also profiled are two prominent individuals, who are associated through the influences they had on one another, the successes they achieved, or the goals they worked toward. Includes recommended readings and web sites"--Provided by publisher.
  Includes bibliographical references and index.
  ISBN-13: 978-0-7166-1827-0
  ISBN-10: 0-7166-1827-3
  1. Chavez, Cesar, 1927--Juvenile literature. 2. Huerta, Dolores, 1930--Juvenile literature. 3. Migrant agricultural laborers--Labor unions--United States--Officials and employees--Biography--Juvenile literature. 4. Mexican American migrant agricultural laborers--Biography--Juvenile literature. 5. United Farm Workers--History--Juvenile literature. 6. Powderly, Terence Vincent, 1849-1924--Juvenile literature. 7. Knights of Labor--History--Juvenile literature. 8. Labor leaders--United States--Biography--Juvenile literature. I. World Book, Inc. II. Title. III. Series.
  HD6509.C48T47 2007
  331.88'13092--dc22
  [B]
                                       2006016502
Printed in the United States of America
1 2 3 4 5 10 09 08 07 06

Contents

Acknowledgments

The publisher gratefully acknowledges the following sources for the photographs in this volume. All maps are the exclusive property of World Book, Inc.

Cover	© Tim Graham, *Evening Standard*/Getty Images
	© Corbis/Bettmann
	© Time Life Pictures/Getty Images
7	© Corbis/Bettmann
12	Library of Congress
19	Granger Collection
20	© Corbis/Bettmann
22	Granger Collection
27	© Time Life Pictures/Getty Images
31	WORLD BOOK map
38-41	Walter Reuther Library from Wayne State University
43	American Museum of American History
49	© Time Life Pictures/Getty Images
51	© Corbis/Bettmann
58	© Paul Fusco, Magnum Photos
63-66	AP/Wide World
69-73	© Corbis/Bettmann
74	© Time Life Pictures/Getty Images
75-77	AP/Wide World
78	© Time Life Pictures/ Getty Images
81	© Hulton Archive/Getty Images
82	© Corbis/Bettmann
85	© Paul Fusco, Magnum Photos
87	© Jose L. Munoz
88	AP/Wide World
91-104	© Time Life Pictures/Getty Images
106	© Amanda Edwards, Getty Images

Preface

Biographical Connections takes a contextual approach in presenting the lives of important people. In each volume, there is a biography of a central figure. This biography is preceded and followed by profiles of other individuals whose lifework connects in some way to that of the central figure. The three subjects are associated through the influences they had on one another, the successes they achieved, or the goals they worked toward. The series includes men and women from around the world and throughout history in a variety of fields.

Terence V. Powderly, Cesar Chavez, and Dolores Huerta dedicated boundless energy to fight for economic power and justice for people often disregarded or considered "invisible" in the United States. This essential but underpaid work force has included recent immigrants, people of color, women, children, and non-English-speakers. Whether in deep, dirty mines or large corporate farm fields, these individuals often labor at dangerous, arduous jobs for long hours without health benefits, job security, or safety standards.

Powderly, Chavez, and Huerta came from working-class backgrounds and understood firsthand the destructive power of racial and class prejudice. In spite of economic hardships during their childhoods, however, all three had important people in their lives who fostered their self-esteem and confidence. They were encouraged as children and later as young adults to read, explore new ideas, and educate themselves even when their formal days of schooling ended.

When Powderly, Chavez, and Huerta grew up, they became anything but invisible. Superlative speechmakers, they used simple, direct rhetoric to reach diverse audiences. Their tireless efforts were aimed at educating, uniting, and organizing fellow workers into labor unions. From 1879 to 1893, Powderly led the Knights of Labor, one of the most important early labor organizations in America. In 1962, more than a half-century later, Chavez and Huerta founded and organized what would become the United Farm Workers of America (UFW), a union dedicated to migrant farm laborers. Chavez led the UFW until his death in 1993. Huerta continues Chavez's legacy as UFW leader while branching off into new frontiers: working for Hispanic American political power by encouraging Hispanic women to run for public office.

Throughout the process of building their unions, Powderly, Chavez, and Huerta used nonviolent means to persuade the public and industrialists of their point of view. These methods included boycotts, picket lines, marches, creation of union members' cooperatives and, in the case of Chavez, fasting.

All three leaders were no strangers to death threats and physical violence from anti-union thugs, corporate connections with local police, and would-be assassins. Sometimes they were viewed as "subversives." Powderly found himself under extreme suspicion by the media and the public, following the bloody Haymarket Riots in 1886. The Federal Bureau of Investigation kept extensive files on Chavez and Huerta, who were both spied upon regularly by government authorities. Chavez had to hire a bodyguard in the 1970's to protect himself from threats. Huerta was beaten in the 1980's by a policeman during a peaceful protest in San Francisco, resulting in several broken ribs and the surgical removal of her damaged spleen.

Yet, in spite of the hardships and personal sacrifices, Powderly, Chavez, and Huerta each demonstrated a remarkable and inspiring tenacity to try to change the world for the betterment of less fortunate individuals. For Huerta, justice is at the crossroads of equality and freedom. Summing up the fundamentally radical message of Chavez and Powderly, she said: "I would like to be remembered as a woman who cares for fellow humans. We must use our lives to make the world a better place to live, not just to acquire things. That is what we are put on the earth for."[1] ■

Terence V. Powderly (1849–1924)

Terence Vincent Powderly led one of the most important early labor organizations in the United States. From 1879 to 1893, he presided over The Noble and Holy Order of the Knights of Labor, the first industrial union to admit all workers—skilled and unskilled, male and female, black and white, immigrant and native-born. Laborers from coal mining to railroad tending and from garment cutting to shoe manufacturing came together in this union.

Powderly's gift was to forcefully and convincingly voice the anguish of abused, forgotten workers. He was convinced that once the "army of the discontented"[1] was brought together, educated, and focused on a course of action, no power could resist it.

Many of Powderly's ideas focused on the unlimited possibilities inherent in an "all-inclusive workers' crusade for empowerment."[2] Powderly's dream has inspired numerous champions for working-class justice, including such individuals as Mexican American labor leaders Cesar Chavez and Dolores Huerta.

EARLY LIFE

Nothing about Terence V. Powderly's humble beginnings hinted at his future fame. He was born in northeastern Pennsylvania on Jan. 22, 1849, in the small, grimy *company town* (a town built by or around a large corporation) of Carbondale—within sight of coal fields, blast furnaces, smokestacks, and slag heaps. The 11th of 12 children, he described himself in his autobiography as "almost the shake of the bag"[3]—that is, so scrawny and sickly that it was doubtful he would survive.

Childhood scarlet fever left Powderly deaf in one ear. Chronic throat and lung ailments plagued him. He was severely nearsighted but could not afford glasses until he was 18. He spent much of his youth fending off local toughs, who made fun of his oversized, hand-me-down clothes, which were originally worn by his seven older brothers. "[M]y childhood," Powderly later recalled, "was not a picnic."[4]

His parents, Terence and Margery ("Madge"), also experienced hardships. Roman Catholic immigrants, they left County Meath, Ireland, for America in 1827, when Margery was pregnant. In his autobiography, Powderly described how his father had been jailed for shooting a rabbit on the estate of Lord Cunningham. Escape to America may have seemed like a good idea. The couple's first child, a girl, was born aboard ship. The three set foot in New York Harbor with one English shilling (about $6 today) to their name.

After working as a farm laborer, Powderly's father settled the family in Carbondale, where they faced anti-Catholic and anti-immigrant sentiment. Imbued with a staunch work ethic, his father found a job as a mine laborer and later became a mining superintendent.

Powderly's mother had a great deal of influence on him. He described her as "a pronounced Abolitionist,"[5] a person who opposed slavery on moral grounds. Powderly, who was his parents' second youngest child, became something of "the golden boy" in the family circle. He had a bright, quick mind and was a voracious reader. In his diary, he recalled how he enjoyed debating politics and philosophy with his older brothers around the kitchen table. He never doubted, he later confessed, that he had the talent and drive to make a name for himself.

EDUCATION AND EARLY UNION INVOLVEMENT

Powderly went to public school in a local church basement until age 13. After that, he went to work with the main employer of his family, the Delaware and Hudson Canal Company (D&H), which was a coal, canal, and railroad firm. Powderly's job was to guard switches along the rail line. After one year at the company, he graduated to train-car examiner. By age 17, he had become apprenticed in the machinist trade with D&H, where he remained dutifully employed for the next three years.

In 1869, when he was 20 years old, he was working in the D&H locomotive shop when a miners' strike shut down the railroad. He lost his job. At that moment, he realized the interdependency of strike action among different trades. To keep afloat financially, he made his way to Scranton, Pennsylvania, an industrial city dominated by the choking fumes of blast furnaces and steel and iron mills. He found employment as a machinist repairing engines, an experience he seemed to have enjoyed. "I never saw the wheels turn under an engine I built without experiencing a feeling of pride," he wrote in his autobiography. "[I]t was my work. . . ."[6]

Like so many ambitious young men of his era, Powderly was a joiner. He became a member of the Workingmen's Benevolent Association, the Ancient Order of Hibernians, and the Irish Land League. Fraternal organizations like these provided a sense of belonging. Special rituals and regular meetings created a kind of haven for friendship, protection, and prestige. In 1871, 22-year-old Powderly became a member of the Machinists and Blacksmiths International Union. The next year, he impressed the other union members so much that they elected him president. This was the first of Powderly's elected union posts.

Powderly seemed determined to master anything he set his sights upon. He signed up for night school and read all the books he could find concerning his trade. He devoured novels, history books, and magazines. He learned to sketch and paint. He wrote poetry. He joined a debating society. He also swore off liquor as a member of a Catholic temperance union. Alcohol, he confided repeatedly in his diary, was a pitfall on the road to success and "a menace to health and steady income."[7]

On Sept. 19, 1872, he married Hannah Dever, the daughter of a Scranton mineworker. During their first year of marriage, Powderly had a good job. He also was improving himself daily as an officer in the union.

Then, exactly one year after Powderly's marriage, disaster struck. On Sept. 19, 1873, a financial panic gripped Wall Street when the New York Stock Exchange reported the collapse of the investment banking firm of Jay Cooke & Company, which floundered after investing too heavily in railroad securities. The resulting Panic of 1873 was followed by a major, decade-long depression, which was the worst economic crisis in United States history up to that point. Like thousands of other workers, Powderly was laid off.

THE WORKING CLASS IN THE GILDED AGE

Powderly was thrown headlong into the increasing sense of desperation that had convulsed much of the working class during the *Gilded Age*. Marked by a shift to a complex, urban culture, this period of wealth and growth lasted roughly from the end of the American Civil War (1860–1865) until 1900. The name "Gilded Age" befit an era in which superficial gloss barely disguised festering social and economic problems just beneath the surface.

Between 1865 and 1917, the population of the United States nearly tripled. More than one-third of the increase came from newly arrived immigrants. While the population boomed, so did manufacturing. Production of coal, pig iron, steel, and refined oil skyrocketed between 1870 and 1900. Railroads expanded at the average rate of about 4,000 miles (6,400 kilometers) of track per year. Consumer goods and food production soared.

Although this tremendous growth benefited the rich, tremendous hardships were created for the ever-expanding mass of working poor. As industries adopted more technology and assembly lines of unskilled laborers to cut costs and improve profits, former craftsmen lost control over tools, knowledge, materials, and wage-bargaining. Twelve-hour work days, poverty-level wages, and dangerous working conditions plagued the majority of laborers, many of whom did not speak English. Jammed into crowded, substandard housing in cities that had polluted air, poor sewage treatment, and little clean running water, the urban poor experienced high incidences of influenza, typhus, yellow fever, and other communicable diseases.

Workers in rural areas were also hard hit during the Gilded Age. Despite the frontier myth of independence, one-fourth of all farmers by 1880 were tenants. (A tenant farmer is a farmer who raises crops or livestock on land that belongs to another person, to whom the tenant pays rent in cash or in a share of the crops or livestock.) In the Deep South more than 80 percent of all African American farmers were subsistence-level *sharecroppers*. (A sharecropper is a person who farms land for the owner in return for part of the crops.) Expensive freight rates, exorbitant credit, and falling commodity prices tremendously hurt poor farmers. Many lost their land and were forced to find work in cities.

In startling contrast to these farmers' fortunes, wealthy industrialists and entrepreneurs—sometimes called "robber barons" because of the way they manipulated the stock market—enjoyed glittering opulence. For example, Cornelius Vanderbilt made his fortune in steamship and railroad lines, as well as in investments in banking and manufacturing. Vanderbilt was worth more than $105 million (about $1.8 billion today) when he died in 1877. That same year, state militia and federal troops were called out to put down a strike of railroad brakemen whose salaries averaged less than $400 (about $7,000 today) per year. Meanwhile, steel manufacturer Andrew Carnegie, one of the wealthiest individuals of his time, collected about $20 million (about $350 million today) annually in untaxed profits.

DEVOTED UNION ACTIVIST

After losing his job, 25-year-old Powderly also lost faith in the future. Eventually, however, the newlywed threw himself with characteristic energy into self-examination. Who was he? What did he need to be a fulfilled human being? Had prejudice against Catholics and Irish immigrants been to blame for his firing? Did he lose his job because he was head of a local union? These were questions with which he struggled.

For many desperate workers, violence against employers

seemed to offer an answer. Powderly was well aware of the effects of violence in Pennsylvania during the 1870's, when the secret society of immigrant Irish coal miners called the Molly Maguires sabotaged mining operations with explosives, killed guards, and made threats against management. After much reflection, Powderly decided on a nonviolent path. In 1874, he made the momentous decision to help other aggrieved working people. To do this, he became increasingly involved in the Machinists and Blacksmiths International Union. By fully embracing this cause, he may have discovered a kind of substitute for his shattered "American dream" of conventional personal success.

Through his union contacts, he was able to find a job as a machinist on the Oil Creek and Allegheny Valley Railroad in Oil City in western Pennsylvania. This support transformed him into a devoted union activist. He quickly worked his way up through the union's ranks. In 1874, he was appointed chief union organizer for the Industrial Brotherhood of western Pennsylvania. Groomed by union officials for leadership because of his eloquence, Powderly once again displayed a single-minded dedication.

During the 1870's, radical railroad workers and miners in Pennsylvania used fires, explosives, and other forms of violence in desperate efforts to win concessions from employers. This 1877 engraving shows a fire destroying a railroad building in Pittsburgh.

His union commitment, however, would not proceed exactly as he had planned. The economic depression continued to tighten its grip on industry. In 1876, Powderly made reckless, stirring speeches inspiring 1,000 shop hands to go on an unauthorized strike against the Delaware, Lackawanna & Western Railroad. The strike failed. The Industrial Brotherhood splintered and disintegrated.

Left without union affiliation, Powderly made a decision that may have seemed of little import at the time. He became active in the Noble and Holy Order of the Knights of Labor, a small, secret fraternal lodge centered in Philadelphia, Pennsylvania. He had been formally initiated into this union in a special ceremony in 1874. Organized in 1869 by Uriah S. Stephens and other Philadelphia tailors, membership in the Knights was open to anyone except bankers, stockbrokers, professional gamblers, lawyers, and those who sold or manufactured liquor.

In 1876, after observing the failures and excesses of the Industrial Brotherhood, Powderly helped organize a local assembly of the Knights in Scranton, Pennsylvania. A year later, he was selected corresponding secretary of the Knights' district assembly, a position he held until 1886. The first four years of his union salary totaled $400 (about $8,200 today), "out of which," he wrote, "I paid all my expenses."[8]

The Knights were decentralized and somewhat disorganized, allowing Powderly and his fellow Knights in Scranton to follow their own local agenda undisturbed. Powderly began to further develop his talents of leadership and speechmaking.

The Knight's policy of secrecy had attracted many members, who feared the wrath of their anti-union employers. Knights of Labor fraternalism rituals reinforced the ideals of freedom of conscience, friendship, harmony, and independence. The Knights' motto, *An injury to one is the concern of all,* insisted on mutual assistance. What made this "humble body with big ideas"[9] unique for its day was flexibility and openness. Founder Stephens wrote, "I can see ahead of me an organization that will include men and women of every craft, creed, and color."[10]

The Knights of Labor reached out to protect immigrant urban

workers, with the exception of the Chinese, who were racially stigmatized by the Knights. The Knights welcomed women, who were becoming a growing labor force, and African Americans, who had been disenfranchised politically and economically as sharecroppers in the South, to set up their own local assemblies.

GRAND MASTER WORKMAN

In January 1879, Powderly traveled to St. Louis, Missouri, where he was elected Grand Worthy Foreman, an honorary post in the Knights. Later that year, Stephens announced his retirement and recommended Powderly as one of two possible successors. Powderly won the election and in 1879 was named Grand Master Workman (renamed General Master Workman after 1883) for a membership that totaled 9,287.

Powderly had been surrounded all his life by struggling immigrants from Ireland and the United Kingdom. With varying degrees of success, these workers had resisted exploitation by large, often distantly managed corporations. Powderly knew firsthand what it was like to be a wageworker who experienced exploitation, danger, and job insecurity. In spite of the frustration he had witnessed, Powderly was committed to avoiding confrontation. Instead, he sought harmony in industrial relations. He disapproved of strikes, partly because he considered them to be too costly for the small benefits they gained.

Powderly pragmatically understood that to attract more Roman Catholic immigrants to the Knights of Labor, the organization would have to change. The Roman Catholic Church disapproved of secrecy and scriptural references in rituals. Powderly began to lobby to have these eliminated so that the Knights would be a public union.

Powderly did not look like the stereotypical union leader. One Chicago newspaperman remarked that he appeared more "like a college professor than one who has swung a hammer."[11] At age 30, he was slender, 5 feet 7 inches (167.5 centimeters) tall, with mild blue eyes and spectacles. He preferred to wear dark, conventional Prince Albert frock coats, shirts with stand-up collars, and ties. A blond, walruslike mustache hid most of his mouth and reached below his dimpled chin before curling upward. His hands were small, his movements graceful, "like a man of good breeding." The same writer claimed that Powderly looked like someone English novelists might select for "poets, gondola scullers, philosophers and heroes crossed in love."[12]

What impressed people most upon meeting Powderly for the first time was his personality. A popular leader, he attracted countless followers largely because of his energy and devotion. He had an extraordinary ability to remember names and faces. A prolific correspondent, he was said to have written more than 75,000 letters, post cards, and telegrams during his tenure as union leader.

Although he was often described as "one of the most stirring men of the day" for his public speeches, Powderly was not an original philosopher. Instead, he had the ability to draw upon and express eloquently the ideas of others, such as when he called for "the war against monopoly" or "the abolition of wage slavery."[13]

"Whether your [labor] society has anything to do with politics or not, politics will have something to do with your society."

Terence V. Powderly

In addition to writing, Powderly spent much of his time traveling to give speeches, to lobby, to attend meetings, and to advise local assemblies. As a result of his staggering workload, he had bouts with health problems. A somewhat high-strung, emotional man, Powderly occasionally experienced exhaustion, melancholy, and *quinsy,* a very sore throat and fever, which forced him to stay in bed for several days at a time. His more morose side seemed to emerge during crises.

POWDERLY THE POLITICIAN

Powderly saw no conflict between simultaneous devotion to union work and local politics. "Whether your [labor] society has anything to do with politics or not, politics will have something to do with your society,"[14] he said.

In 1876, three years before he was elected Grand Master Workman of the Knights of Labor, Powderly invited labor leaders from around the United States to speak in Scranton. He worked tirelessly during the U.S. presidential election that year to coordinate canvassers and poll watchers for the Greenback Party. Although the party lost that election miserably, Powderly emerged as an influential and popular personality with many Irish Americans and Catholics. He was elected mayor of Scranton on the Greenback-Labor ticket in February 1878 and was reelected in 1880 and 1882. In 1882, he was nominated by the Greenback-Labor Party to run for Pennsylvania's lieutenant governor, but he declined the nomination.

GROWTH AND CHALLENGES WITH THE KNIGHTS

Powderly spent a great deal of his time on extensive speaking tours, "preaching the gospel of proletarian self-help"[15] across the country. (*Proletarian* refers to the lowest class in economic and social status.) Powderly saw his job as educating those working people who had developed a crippling sense of fatalism. "There are men and whole communities," Powderly wrote,

"No strike can hit a blow sufficiently hard to break the hold with which unproductive capital to-day grasps labor by the throat."

Terence V. Powderly, in *Journal of United Labor,* February 1883

"who have from early youth been taught to believe that everything that happens to them, whether good or bad, was ordained of heaven, and that no effort on their part could, or should, change the course of events into a different channel."[16]

Wherever he went, Powderly attempted to learn about local issues so he could identify those causes that potential Knights members could work on together. In 1885, he made a grueling 36-day, 24-city tour of the South. He spoke from Richmond, Virginia, to Memphis, Tennessee, and numerous crossroads villages in between. At each stop, he sought to educate the "audience about the power of collective action to win concrete results."[17]

The South lacked a trade-union tradition. In addition, the docile, unorganized Southern labor force was plagued with a long-standing tradition of rampant racism. These challenges notwithstanding,

Powderly found a way to convince audiences made up of either whites or African Americans that "politicians have kept the white and black men of the South apart, while crushing both," he said. "Our aim shall be to educate both and elevate them by bringing them together."[18] Instead of losing white Knights, as some union officials had predicted, Powderly's tour set off an explosion of organizing activity in Richmond that brought the two racial groups together for the first time to flex "collective muscles."[19]

Leading such a far-flung, decentralized organization with so many different goals was not easy. One historian called Powderly's job "a storm center in the camp of organized labor. [Powderly] was attacked from all sides—by trade-unionists, fellow Knights, employers, reformers, politicians, and clerics."[20] Yet he did not give up the fight.

His goal was first to build consensus among members by identifying the majority opinion on key issues. He saw programs of action emerging from the bottom up. One phrase he emphasized over and over again in his speeches was, "Educate yourself as to what you want." He never pretended to have all the answers. "The great question of labor," he said, "requires for its solution a greater mind than mine."[21]

EARLY STRIKES

By 1880, the Knights' General Assembly had worked out a clearly defined strike procedure to curb unauthorized walk-outs by members. Powderly saw his role and that of other officers as offering financial and moral assistance during a strike, which he considered a weapon of last resort. "No strike," he wrote, "can hit a blow sufficiently hard to break the hold with which unproductive capital to-day grasps labor by the throat."[22]

Although he tried to consistently counsel arbitration and conciliation as alternatives, local Knights initiated strikes—sometimes unexpectedly. In 1883, a group of Knights who were telegraphers walked off the job for Western Union Telegraph Company, which was owned by Jay Gould, an American financier who, by 1880, controlled more than 8,000 miles (12,800 kilometers) of railroad track. Nicknamed the "Wizard of Wall Street," Gould had become a multimillionaire by using business tactics that his critics viewed as dishonest.

The strike by workers against Western Union failed. Miners' strikes ended in similar defeats in Pennsylvania, Ohio, and Indiana. Again, separate Knights' strikes sputtered out without success for iron molders, carpet weavers, and textile spinners. In spite of this poor record, Knights' membership climbed from more than 71,000 in 1884 to more than 111,000 in 1885. New members included such disenfranchised fringe groups as Marxists, socialists, and *anarchists*. The latter group sought to abolish all government authority.

The Knights had small but important successes at this time, including the creation of their first African American local, which was formed by a group of coal miners in Ottumwa, Iowa. Another success was their first all-women local, organized for shoe workers in Philadelphia in 1881. Although some male Knights felt that women could not be trusted with the secrets of the Knights, Powderly insisted that women be allowed to create assemblies. He personally initiated Frances Willard, founder of the Women's Temperance Union, and suffragette Susan B. Anthony. (A *suffragette* was someone who fought for the right of women to vote.)

SUCCESS AND TRAGEDY

Gould seemed nearly unstoppable as he built his empire of western railway lines throughout the 1880's. Among his many holdings were the Denver Pacific, Kansas Pacific, Missouri Pacific, and Union Pacific. The Knights of Labor achieved national recognition in 1885 during the first successful unilateral strike against Gould's Southwest Railway Conglomerate.

In October 1884, Gould had announced a 10-percent reduction in shopworkers' wages on the conglomerate's Missouri, Kansas, and Texas Railroad. In February 1885, he declared another wage slash for workers on the Wabash line. A strike broke out in Moberly, Missouri, and quickly spread through three Gould lines: the Missouri, Kansas, and Texas; the Wabash; and the Missouri

Pacific—representing a total of nearly 20,000 miles (32,000 kilometers) of railroad track.

On July 25, 1885, Gould's empire nearly staggered to a halt when the Knights of Labor passed a resolution requesting that the governors of Illinois, Indiana, Missouri, and Kansas intervene in the dispute. At the same time, the order told all of its members who were still working on the Wabash and Union Pacific lines to not handle any Wabash rolling stock.

With Gould on his knees, Powderly stepped in and agreed that no future strikes would be called until a conference with the railroad officials could be held. The strike was called off. This was a major victory for the Knights of Labor. The "Wizard of Wall Street" had been forced to the labor bargaining table for the first time. Furthermore, two giant railroad lines had been forced to recognize the Knights.

Machinist Frank J. Farrell, standing right, introduces Powderly, standing left, to the 10th annual convention of the Knights of Labor in Richmond, Virginia, in this 1886 engraving.

Although there were a number of loopholes in the Knights' agreement with Gould that would later come back to haunt the union, this was a moment of glory for Powderly. The Knights now had enough credibility to forcefully lobby the U.S. Congress on a number of important causes, including an end to convict labor, the establishment of a bureau of labor statistics, and the elimination of the industrywide use of immigrant strikebreakers.

Gould's defeat, one historian wrote, created a stampede to the Knights of Labor that was "likened to the faithful embracing a savior."[23] In 1886, Knights membership grew almost seven times in size, to a total of nearly 730,000 from about 111,000 the year before. Local assemblies of the Knights were organized in virtually every large industrial city in the United States and Canada. Membership stretched from the Deep South to Canada, from East Coast cities to ports along the California coast. Members came from rural backwater villages and busy urban centers. Throughout the United States in 1886, political candidates from the Knights won several local and state offices.

The Knights, the "champion of the underdog," gained such a great diversity of new members that many of them voiced conflicting demands. The rapid growth and ensuing organizational chaos convinced Powderly in 1886 to call a moratorium on chartering new local assemblies.

The swelling ranks of Knights members in 1886 coincided with the rapid growth of other labor movements as workers sensed new power. The Federation of Organized Trades and Labor Unions of the United States and Canada (FOOTALU) called on all U.S. workers to stage a nationwide general strike on May 1, 1886. FOOTALU, which competed with the Knights for the representation of skilled

Women delegates to the annual convention of the Knights of Labor in 1886 pose for a group portrait. The Knights welcomed women, who were becoming a growing labor force in the United States in the late 1800's.

trade workers, demanded an eight-hour workday. A 10-hour workday was typical at the time.

Months before, Powderly had sent a letter to Knights members suggesting that they exercise caution and not participate in the May 1 general strike. Nearly 4,000 assemblies endorsed Powderly's idea of restraint. However, the organization soon found itself embroiled in internal fighting and name-calling when a situation in Chicago became an unexpected flash point.

THE HAYMARKET RIOT AND AFTERMATH

Nearly 80,000 trade-union members went on strike in Chicago on May 1, 1886. Two days later, the strike widened to include the McCormick Reaper Works, which was the Chicago industrial plant of McCormick Harvesting Machine Company. When *scabs* (strikebreakers) arrived, a fight broke out between the strikers and scabs, resulting in the deaths of several workers. Angry labor organizers, including anarchists, called for armed action by workers. Word went out that a rally would be held on May 4 at Haymarket Square in Chicago to protest police actions against strikers at the McCormick industrial plant.

When police tried to break up the Haymarket Square rally, an unidentified individual hurled a homemade bomb. A riot broke out. Police and members of the mob exchanged gunfire. Seven policemen and one civilian were fatally wounded. Countless bystanders were injured.

Newspapers were filled with stories about the Haymarket Riot. On Aug. 20, 1886, eight anarchists were convicted of conspiracy against the police. Although none of them was found guilty of throwing the bomb or causing any of the deaths, seven were sentenced to death. The eighth was sent to prison. In 1887, four of the seven condemned men were hanged, one committed suicide, and the remaining two had their sentences *commuted* (reduced) to life in prison. Six years later, the three imprisoned anarchists were pardoned by the Illinois governor, who declared that the evidence had been insufficient to support the charges against them.

A satirical cartoon published in 1886 depicts Powderly giving the back of his hand to both a scab *(strikebreaker) and an employer. The original caption, purporting to quote Powderly, read, "We work not selfishly for ourselves alone, but extend the hand of fellowship to all mankind."*

In the wake of the Haymarket Riot, antilabor sentiment increased among the general population in the United States, especially in regard to anarchists, who many people viewed as foreign "agitators" and outsiders. Powderly, who had never publicly supported the strike or the pardon of the so-called "agitators," faced intense criticism from many impatient union leaders and rank-and-file members, as well as much of the public. Many people felt that the "noisy, tempestuous, strike-happy" Knights had somehow been responsible for the Haymarket tragedy. Meanwhile, Powderly continued to counsel caution.

Later in 1886, when the Knights called a second strike against Gould, the action failed miserably. The business community closed ranks and began firing people suspected of being members of the Knights. No arbitration was offered. Setbacks in other industries, including meat packing, textiles, and shoe manufacturing seemed to seal the Knights' doom. As Knights members dropped out of the organization or stopped paying dues, the labor union experienced a cash crisis. The union could not afford to pay staff or lecturers or to keep up a strike defense fund. In 1890, a disastrous strike against the New York Central and Hudson River Railroad effectively destroyed the Knights' remaining power in the industrial Northeast.

As the urban industrial areas experienced a steady decline of union support, rural areas remained small, steadily growing bastions of union activity. In 1892, 82 Knights took part in a political convention in Omaha, Nebraska, that led to the founding of the labor-oriented Populist Party. The following year, Knights of Labor agrarians teamed up with the remaining urban radicals and began to attempt to remove Powderly from power.

Powderly's leadership had been steadily floundering since 1890. Involved with too many organizations and projects, he found himself overwhelmed. In 1889, he published the labor history, *Thirty Years of Labor,* in an attempt to describe "the story of one movement in a given direction for a short period of time. . . ."[24] In 1893, he finally conceded that he had to resign because the Knights' General Executive Board had become antagonistic to his policies.

NEW DIRECTIONS

After giving up leadership of the Knights of Labor, Powderly's life turned in a new direction. In 1894, 45-year-old Powderly became a lawyer. Three years later, he was practicing law before the Supreme Court of Pennsylvania.

In addition to his law career, he became involved again in public service. He was appointed Commissioner-General of Immigration by President William McKinley, serving in that position from 1897 to 1902. Powderly also held various other government posts in the Department of Commerce under President Theodore Roosevelt. Simultaneously, he tried his hand at running several business ventures, including a coal company and a real estate business. However, his commercial ventures did not prove to be successful.

Powderly wrote for a number of magazines and official government publications. In 1921, he completed his autobiography, *The Path I Trod*, which he had begun many years earlier. As he explained in a letter to a friend in 1907, "I have not been understood by many and I want to prepare this to leave after me so that I shall be able to give a reason for what I did . . . so that my real self will be known. . . ."[25] The autobiography would not be published until 1940.

Powderly's wife, Hannah, died in 1901. The couple had no children. He married his second wife, Emma Frickenscher, 18 years later, on March 13, 1919, when he was 70. Emma had been his secretary at the Knights of Labor, and she was a woman whom Powderly considered to be invaluable.

Powderly succumbed to respiratory and throat ailments five years into his second marriage. He died at home on June 24, 1924, in Washington, D.C., at age 75. His death attracted almost no notice from the mainstream press. By the time he passed away, the Knights of Labor had few remaining members. The last official Knights of Labor convention occurred in Boston in 1932.

AN INSPIRATION TO OTHERS

Mary Harris Jones, who was nicknamed "Mother Jones," was a long-time labor activist who had been inspired by the Knights of Labor during the early days of her career. Expressing her sense of loss at the death of Powderly, she declared that Powderly was "the one faithful friend I had."[26] Although Powderly's labor organization eventually failed, the idea that the world might be improved through inclusive, cooperative effort among the forces of labor remained an inspiration to Jones and others.

Powderly's vision would continue to resonate with many people striving for working-class justice. At a time of turmoil and unrest, hopelessness and poverty, Powderly and the Knights of Labor had taken far-sighted positions on diverse issues—abolition of the wage system, convict labor, cooperative production, currency reform, equal rights for women, race relations, and religious tolerance.

The Knights of Labor was the largest labor organization of its kind in a period when the number of American workers was skyrocketing. In 1860, there were about 5.3 million nonagricultural wage earners; by 1900, there were more than 17.4 million. During the two decades before 1900, the United States experienced 2,378 strikes involving nearly 6 million workers. Many of these strikes were the direct result of Knights activities.

Looking back on the beginning of labor's rise and Powderly's ascendancy in the Knights, Mother Jones described the early years of the Knights as a special time of seemingly limitless possibilities. "Those were the days of sacrifice for the cause of labor," she later wrote in her autobiography. "Those were the days when we had no halls, when there were no high-salaried officers, no feasting with the enemies of labor. Those were the days of the martyrs and the saints."[27] ■

Chronology of Chavez's life

1927   born on March 21 in Yuma, Arizona

1944   family moves to San Jose barrio of Sal Si Puedes; enlists in
        United States Navy

1946   honorably discharged from Navy

1948   marries Helen Fabela on October 22

1949   Fernando, the first of eight children, is born to Cesar and Helen

1952   recruited by Fred Ross to work in the Community Service Organization
        (CSO) of the Industrial Areas Foundation; serves as chairman of CSO
        voter registration drive

1958   organizes CSO chapter in Oxnard, California

1959   becomes executive director of CSO

1962   works as a director for the U.S. Peace Corps in South America; founds
        Farm Workers Association as an independent farmworkers union
        (name later changed to National Farm Workers Association [NFWA])

1965   calls for first boycott of grapes, to put pressure on growers to sign con-
        tract with NFWA

1966   organizes 300-mile (480-kilometer) march in California that receives
        widespread national attention; merges NFWA with Agricultural Workers
        Organizing Committee to form United Farm Workers Organizing
        Committee (name later changed to United Farm Workers of America)

1968   stages 25-day fast in support of nonviolence

1973   fasts for 3 ½ weeks against Arizona law that outlaws secondary boycotts
        and harvest-time strikes

1974   presented with Nonviolent Peace Prize by Coretta Scott King

1975   march against E. & J. Gallo Winery and lettuce boycott prompt
        California Governor Edmund G. "Jerry" Brown, Jr., to sign California
        Agricultural Labor Relations Act

1984   final boycott of grapes, to protest use of agricultural pesticides

1990   awarded Aguila Azteca, highest civilian award in Mexico

1993   dies in sleep on April 23 in Yuma

Cesar Chavez (1927–1993)

Overcoming enormous social, economic, and political obstacles, Cesar Estrada Chavez *(SHAH vehz)* committed his life to working as a union organizer and spokesperson for the poor—especially fellow Mexican American migrant farm laborers. Following the path set by a number of other social reformers of the 20th century, Chavez used nonviolent actions, such as boycotts and marches, to achieve the aims of *La Causa* (The Cause).

Like 19th-century American labor leader Terence Vincent Powderly, Chavez was an accomplished, inspiring speaker and charismatic leader. In the late 1960's and early 1970's, a wide cross section of Americans lent their support to the United Farm Workers Organizing Committee (UFWOC), an organization formed by the merger of the Agricultural Workers Organizing Committee (AWOC) with Chavez's National Farm Workers Association. The UFWOC became the United Farm Workers of America (UFW) in 1972. The UFW was one of the first unions dedicated to justice for Mexican and Mexican American farmworkers. Chavez became a symbol of pride and hope in the *Chicano* (Mexican American) movement.

Chavez's major goal was to win for farmworkers the right to organize on their own behalf. However, severe roadblocks stood in the way of his tireless efforts.

Seasonal farm laborers are in large part illiterate. They comprise mostly minority groups. Many do not speak English. They are constantly on the move. Migrant workers—some illegally residing in the United States—have traditionally avoided protest out of the belief that such action would mean starvation, hopelessness, or possible deportation.

Chavez and his union were up against large agribusinesses run by powerful vegetable, fruit, grain, and cotton growers. Since the early 1900's, strikes, protests, and union organizing efforts of migrant workers had been systematically destroyed by large-scale growers.

Chavez also faced legal barriers created by the U.S. Congress. Since the Great Depression, a period of severe, worldwide economic hardship during the 1930's, farmworkers had been excluded from labor protections by the National Labor Relations Act of 1935 (also known as the Wagner Act).

Chavez was able to overcome these roadblocks. The epic struggle for labor rights and justice continues today in the hands of both new leaders and such veteran organizers as Dolores Huerta.

Chapter 1: The Early Years

Yuma, Arizona, is a small, sun-bleached desert town in the North Gila River Valley near the borders of California and Mexico. On March 21, 1927, the day that Cesar Estrada Chavez was born, the swift, deep Colorado River ran wild past the town on its way deep into Mexico. Fruit growers and orchard owners had not yet dammed and diverted the river north of Yuma, near California's Imperial Valley.

Cesar, the second of five surviving children of Librado and Juana Chavez, was in many ways like that river. As a young boy he was described as shy but strong-willed. One day in school, he was so strongly opposed to sitting beside his older sister that even his teacher could not prevent him from running out of the classroom.

Freedom was what he recalled most strongly about his grandparents' nearby 160-acre (64-hectare) farm, where he and his younger brother, Richard, roamed and explored, building forts and swimming in the drainage canals. Chavez also was allowed to visit his parents' three businesses in town: a grocery store, above which was the family home; an automotive garage; and a pool hall, where the clients included dozens of Chavez relatives.

"I had more happy moments as a child than unhappy moments," Chavez later recalled. "We were a very close family."[1] Almost every evening in the summer, his large clan of cousins, aunts, and uncles gathered for barbecues where they drank lemonade and ate watermelon and fresh ears of corn that were roasted in a fire hole. Chavez and his cousins often slept outdoors under mosquito netting and listened to the grown-ups tell ghost stories or daring tales of adventure about relatives who had worked in mines or who fought in the Mexican Revolution of 1910.

One of his favorite stories was how his paternal grandfather, Cesario, for whom he was named, had escaped in the 1880's from a *hacienda* (large farm) in Chihuahua, Mexico, where he had been kept as a kind of lifelong servant. "Papa Chayo," as he was later nicknamed, managed to escape his bondage and made his way to the United States. There he worked in the mines, saving money little by little to buy his own land. The early stories about his grandfather impressed young Chavez, who was amazed that workers on the prison-like hacienda could not speak out for their rights.

Chavez's parents were important influences on him. From his father, "a large, powerful man nearly 6 feet [180 centimeters] tall and weighing more than 200 pounds [90 kilograms], with huge hands that were strong and clumsy,"[2] Chavez said he learned to stand up for his rights. From his mother, who was barely 5 feet (150 centimeters) tall, he heard countless *dichos* (proverbs) about nonviolence. She was a deeply religious woman—though "not a fanatic," Chavez said later in life. Her favorite dichos included: "What you do to others, others do to you" and "He who holds the cow being killed sins as much as he who kills her."[3]

Much of his mother's *consejos* (advice) was about not fighting. "Despite a culture where you're not a man if you don't fight back," explained Chavez: "[my mother] would say, 'No, it's best to turn the other cheek. God gave you senses like eyes and a mind and tongue, and you can get out of anything.'" His mother's favorite reminder: "It takes two to fight, and one can't do it alone." When Chavez grew up and read the works of Gandhi and St. Francis, he realized that his mother, too, had promoted the idea of nonviolence in word and deed.

Although Chavez's mother was illiterate, she was very wise, particularly when it came to instilling values in her children. Being selfish was one thing his mother did not allow. Chavez recalled how she made him and his brothers and sisters share everything they had. "If we had an apple or a tiny piece of candy," he said, "we had to cut it into five pieces."[4]

Throughout his childhood, he and his brothers and sisters were instructed in religion by their beloved paternal grandmother, nicknamed Mama Tella. As a young girl, Mama Tella worked as a servant in a convent in Mexico. She was the only one of Chavez's grandparents who could read and write in Spanish and Latin. Chavez's Roman Catholic faith would become of enormous importance in sustaining him as he grew older and became involved in union organizing. As he later explained: "To me, religion is a most beautiful thing. And over the years, I have come to realize that all religions are beautiful. . . . For me, Christianity happens to be a natural source of faith . . . [Christ] was very clear in what he meant and knew exactly what he was after. He was extremely radical, and he was for social change."[5]

THE GREAT DEPRESSION

Life took an unexpected turn for Chavez and his family in 1929, the year the Great Depression began in the United States with the crash of the New York Stock Market. In the Depression, which continued through the end of the 1930's, banks, factories, and shops closed, and farms halted production. Millions of Americans were left penniless and jobless.

Large numbers of unemployed urban workers in the United States drifted west and south into the migrant farm labor market, where they

The life and work of Cesar Chavez took place mostly in the state of California, where the Chavez family moved (from Arizona) in the late 1930's.

hoped to find work. With the growing availability of drifting white workers, U.S. growers put pressure on Mexicans of all backgrounds to leave the country. In a mass deportation of alleged *aliens* (noncitizens) conducted by the U.S. government, about 300,000 Mexicans and Mexican Americans were herded across the border to Mexico.

Meanwhile, years of drought had led to devastating dust storms in Colorado, Kansas, Oklahoma, New Mexico, and Texas. Hungry and desperate for work, poor farmers from these Dust Bowl states headed west to California in boxcars and jalopies. The flood of workers by the tens of thousands further depressed wages and brought local welfare systems to the verge of collapse.

"Suddenly two cars bore down on us. . . . Uniformed men piled out of the cars and surrounded ours. We were half-asleep, all scared, and crying."

Cesar Chavez, describing an experience his family had with the border patrol when he was 11 years old

For the Chavez family, which was surrounded by a network of relatives, and for whom their grandparents' farm was always available to meet their food needs, the Depression seemed a distant problem at first. They had always been accustomed to making do with little and they shared what they had. Then, in 1933, the worst drought in more than five decades shriveled the Colorado River. The irrigation ditches for the Chavez family farm dried up. Without rain or irrigation water, crops perished. Like others who lived in the Gila River Valley, the Chavez family soon found itself without income. The garage, grocery store, and pool hall had been operating on a casual system of I.O.U.'s from friends and family. Now, no one could pay his or her debts. Yuma businesses were boarding up their windows and doors.

The crisis finally hit the Chavez family when their property and water tax bill of more than $4,000 came due for their 80-acre (32-hectare) piece of land. Chavez's father had no money to pay the taxes. A neighboring farmer, who was interested in taking over the property, succeeded in using political clout to block a bank loan that would have helped the Chavez family buy time. At this point, Librado Chavez had lost his businesses and was in danger of losing the family farm, as well.

MOVE TO CALIFORNIA

In a desperate attempt to pay off his debt, Librado Chavez drove to California in 1938 to try to get a job. When he finally found work, he sent for his wife and five children to leave the farm and join him in California. The children, ranging in age from 4 to 13, piled into a car with their mother and two cousins. The cousins shared the driving.

At first, the journey west from Arizona seemed like an exciting expedition to 11-year-old Cesar, who had never before been so far away from Yuma. Night fell as the family neared Oxnard, California, northwest of Los Angeles, when Chavez was abruptly woken from his sleep by glaring floodlights. He later recalled: "Suddenly two cars bore down on us. . . . Uniformed men piled out of the cars and surrounded ours. We were half-asleep, all scared, and crying. It was the border patrol, our first experience with any kind of law. Roughly, they asked for identification, our birth certificates, proof of American citizenship. My mother must have died a hundred times that night."[6]

The family was questioned for hours. The humiliation had a lasting impact on Chavez, who later recalled how the officers seemed to believe that a Mexican American family was automatically suspect and therefore considered fair game for abuse. "In their minds," he said, "'If he's Mexican, don't trust him.'"[7]

By the time they reached Oxnard, the only place they could find to live was in a dilapidated shack. The job that Chavez's father found paid so poorly that the family had to scrounge for wild mustard greens to have something to eat. Eventually, relatives back in Yuma sent a few dollars so that Chavez's family could buy gas to make it to Los Angeles. For the next few weeks, the family drifted east, following the cotton harvest near Brawley, California. The pay for working the harvest was so bad, however, that they eventually gave up and returned penniless to Yuma.

This disastrous experience marked the end of Chavez's carefree childhood. His world had changed irrevocably. His father in desperation even traveled to Phoenix to plead his case before the Arizona governor, but there seemed no hope. Chavez was 11 years old when the deputy sheriff arrived at their farm and served his family with a final eviction notice. The notice stated that the family must leave the property or go to jail. Chavez's mother came out of the house in tears. Meanwhile, Chavez and his brothers and sisters were confused and worried.

After several visits from the deputy, the family finally packed up their few belongings into a 1930 Studebaker automobile. They had only $40 to their name. Chavez and his brothers and sisters and sobbing mother watched as a tractor bulldozer drove onto the property, knocked down precious trees, and flattened the hand-hewn corral where Chavez and his brother had spent so much time riding horses and chasing calves. After leveling the land, the bulldozer shoved dirt into the dried-up irrigation canal. The horrifying sight meant that there could be no return.

"We left everything behind," Chavez remembered. "Left chickens and cows and horses and all implements. Things belonging to my father's family and my mother's as well. Everything."[8]

FAMILY OF MIGRANT WORKERS

It was at that moment that the Chavez family joined the ranks of Americans cast adrift by the Great Depression. The Chavezes had officially become part of the flood of migrant workers who had been driven from their land and forced on the road to find work on factory farms, many of which were run by absentee landlords.

"We had never worked for anybody else. We never lived away from our home," wrote Chavez's older sister, Rita Medina Chavez. "Here we come to California, and we were lucky we got a tent. Most of the time we were living under a tree, with just a canvas on top of us, and sometimes in the car."[9]

For the next several months, the family followed the harvest from the carrot fields near Brawley, California, to other vegetable fields outside of Oxnard. The Chavezes moved north and east up the San Joaquin Valley, eventually reaching the grape harvests near Fresno, California. The family was approached by a *labor contractor*, an individual who worked for a grower to hire the cheapest labor possible. The contractor offered to house the family in an old camp near the grape fields. Every week, he made excuses for not paying them. One morning, at the end of the season, the contractor disappeared. The family was left without a cent. This experience with a corrupt labor contractor was one that Chavez would never forget.

In the fall of 1939, the family began picking cotton near Mendota, west of Fresno, in the San Joaquin Valley. Cotton was a crop that promised to provide good money if the picker was fast enough and strong enough to harvest 300 to 400 pounds (135 to 180 kilograms) of it a day. However, by the time the Chavez family arrived, there was little cotton left to harvest.

That winter, they lived in a small tar-paper-and-wood cabin that had a single electrical outlet. A communal outhouse and outdoor faucets for water were shared by everyone. A company store sold high-priced groceries and supplies to its employees on credit, which left many families continually in debt. When the winter ended, the Chavez family barely had enough money to fill their tank with gas and drive to the next place where they could beg for work.

Traveling from camp to camp meant that there was no sense of permanence and no sense of home. Chavez and his brothers and sisters had lost not only a sense of continuity and predictability, but also a sense of spaciousness. There was nowhere for them to play or run free. Everywhere they looked were signs that said, "No trespassing." "I felt caged,"[10] Chavez remembered later. "I bitterly missed the ranch. Maybe that is when the rebellion started. Some [people] had been born into the migrant stream. But we had been on the land, and I knew a different way of life. We were poor, but we had liberty. The migrant is poor, but he has no freedom."[11]

Every member of the family had to help if he or she could. Speed, know-how, care, and strength were necessary to successfully survive in the fields. Chavez and his family rose before dawn to prune grapevines and wrap them around wires. They became skilled at picking the right fruit—not too ripe, not too green. As they moved from crop to crop, children and grown-ups alike tended and harvested apricots, beans, berries, broccoli, cabbage, carrots, cherries, corn, cotton, grapes, lettuce, melons, peas, plums, sugar beets, tomatoes, and walnuts. Chavez recalled that harvesting broccoli was an especially difficult task for children. Because the broccoli harvest was in the winter, he and his brothers and sisters would slip on the cold, wet ground. Mud sucked off their shoes. Their fingers went numb from the cold as they sliced the tough broccoli stalks with knives.

For the next 10 years, Chavez and his family followed the stream of migrant labor from job to job, harvest to harvest. One of the most physically grueling jobs was thinning lettuce or cantaloupe with a short-handled hoe. This job required the laborer to bend low and claw row after row of the crop with the hoe. "You have to walk twisted, as you're stooped over, facing the row, and walking perpendicular,"[12] he said, recalling the excruciating back pain that left many farmworkers almost crippled. In 1942, 15-year-old Chavez and his family worked with short-handled hoes in cantaloupe fields. He and his brothers and sisters were paid 8 cents an hour; his parents made 12 cents. At that point there were five workers in the family: his parents, 17-year-old Rita, 15-year-old Cesar, and Richard, 14. The two younger children, Vicky, 8, and Lenny, 6, stayed in the car.

Contractors often charged the workers considerable amounts—for food or water or to drive them to the fields. Some workers had to rent their own bushel baskets or hampers. These expenses cut deeply into a day's pay. To help earn extra money, Chavez and his brother Richard shelled walnuts, chopped firewood, and searched the sides of the roads and railroad tracks for cigarette wrappers. At the time, tinfoil was used to package cigarettes. Little by little, the two boys collected an 18-pound (8.1-kilogram) ball of metal foil. They sold this to a junk dealer, who gave them enough cash to purchase two sweatshirts and a pair of tennis shoes.

Chavez and his brother swept out a movie theater for the payment of a nickel a day and a chance to see their favorite series, *The Lone Ranger*. They cleaned up boxing and wrestling rings after Friday night matches to make 10 cents. "We were hustling all the time, working not for ourselves but for the family,"[13] Chavez later wrote.

RACIAL AND ECONOMIC DISCRIMINATION

Chavez's experience in the fields and on odd jobs in small towns exposed him for the first time to the enormity of a new kind of racial and economic discrimination—something he had been protected from on the isolated farm in Yuma. In Brawley, California, when Chavez was about 12 years old, he and his brother Richard shined shoes and sold newspapers to make money. They went to Mass early, then set up their stand on the streets in the "Anglo" (white Americans of other than Spanish or Mexican descent) section of town. When they finished their work, they gave their shoeshine kits to a Chinese man who owned a store.

One day, after shining shoes, they went to a diner on the Anglo side of town. There was a sign on the window that said "White trade only," but the boys went in anyway. "We had heard they had these big hamburgers and we wanted one. There was a blonde, blue-eyed girl behind the counter, a beauty. She asked what we wanted—real tough, you know?—and when we ordered a hamburger, she said, 'We don't sell to Mexicans,' and she laughed when she said it. She enjoyed doing that, laughing at us. We went out, but I was really mad, enraged. It had to do with my manhood."[14]

So much movement from town to town, crop to crop, meant that Chavez and his brothers and sisters were never in one school for very long. Chavez later could not even recall exactly how many schools he attended, but the number was probably more than 30.

Both of Chavez's parents were raised in Arizona, which had been part of Mexico more than a generation earlier, and they both spoke Spanish, not English. Chavez and his brothers and sisters grew up with both languages in Yuma. In the Yuma schools, they had been scolded, smacked on the hand, or publicly humiliated if they used Spanish. Chavez once had to wear a sign around his neck that read, "I am a clown; I speak Spanish."[15]

As migrant workers moving from place to place, Chavez and his siblings were tormented by some students in school because they were so poor. They often came to school shoeless or wearing the same sweatshirts day after day. In California, they were persecuted for having dark skin and Indian features. Although not part of state

Chavez poses with his diploma upon his graduation from eighth grade in Brawley, California, when he was 15 years old.

law, every town had developed its own form of segregation in theaters, schools, stores, restaurants, and hotels.

"In integrated schools, where we were the only Mexicans," Chavez remembered, "we were like monkeys in a cage. There were lots of racist remarks that still hurt my ears when I think of them. And we couldn't do anything except sit there and take it."[16] Indifference and open hostility from teachers and principals were often encountered by Chavez and his brothers and sisters. From his experience in segregated schools, he learned what it was like to be classified as inferior and made to feel excluded.

While in Brawley, California, 15-year-old Chavez managed to complete eighth grade. After graduation, he decided he was finished with school. His mother protested his decision, but Chavez was determined to help earn money for his family full-time. His father had been in a car accident and his mother was too frail, he believed, to work in the fields anymore. He could read and write in English and Spanish. What else did he need to know? Much later, Chavez would regret his lost years of education.

In spite of racial and economic prejudice, Chavez recalled with a kind of pride that his was "probably one of the strikingest families in California."[17] His father, though a reserved man, refused to put up with discrimination and bad treatment in the field. Once, during the height of a cotton harvest in the San Joaquin Valley, the entire family dropped their tools and walked off the job because they suspected that the foreman was purposefully underweighing their produce. In another incident, during Santa Clara's cherry harvest, the piece rate dropped from 2 cents to 1 ½ cents per pound, causing his family to protest. "We were the first ones to leave the fields if anybody shouted *Huelga* [strike]. . . . It didn't come to us because we knew anything about labor," Chavez later said. "It came to us because it was the right thing to do."[18]

There was a kind of pride involved in walking off the job when the conditions were too awful or unfair. "Lose a day's pay, or two, but we felt we had kept something that belonged to us . . . our dignity,"[19] said Chavez. He later reflected that because his family had once owned land and businesses and had experienced the independence of being their own bosses, they had a kind of resilience and spirit that many other migrant laborers lacked.

YOUTHFUL REBELLION

A sense of rebellion began to percolate to the surface when Chavez was a teen-ager. His family had often ended up in Delano, California, a small town in the rich agricultural San Joaquin Valley. The Delano *barrio* (neighborhood) in which the family often stayed was a tough neighborhood. It was here that Chavez started sporting the Mexican American *pachuco* look. This consisted of a "zoot suit," which was a flamboyant long coat with baggy, pegged pants. The look was completed with a flat, wide-brimmed "porkpie" hat and thick-soled shoes.

"Pachuco" is a word of uncertain origin that referred to not only a clothing style, but also to the Spanish slang spoken by those who wore the rebellious style. The style, which was considered dangerous, often invited harassment from police. The pachuco look marked victims of racially motivated beatings by white servicemen in Los Angeles during the so-called Zoot Suit riots, which took place in June 1943. A Los Angeles ordinance was eventually passed making it a misdemeanor to wear this clothing.

In 1944, the Chavez family moved to the San Jose barrio called *Sal Si Puedes* (literally translated as "get out if you can"). One way to escape the grinding poverty of the tough, violent barrio and the brutality of work in the fields was to enlist in the U.S. armed forces. Overruling his parents' objections in 1944, 17-year-old Chavez enlisted in the Navy during World War II (1939–1945) for a two-year stint. He found a world that he had not known existed. When he arrived in the San Diego boot camp, he discovered that other people suffered prejudice because of their nationality or language. "I saw this white kid fighting because someone had called him a Polack,"[20] he wrote.

During his service in the Navy, Chavez traveled to the South Pacific and later to Guam, where he worked as a painter, which was the only job besides deck hand available to Mexican Americans. Later, he described his time in the Navy as the worst years of his life because of the "super authority that somehow somebody has the right to move you around like a piece of equipment. It's worse than being in prison."[21]

One day when he came home on leave to Delano, he went in his regular clothing to a movie theater, where one-quarter of the seats were set aside for Mexicans, blacks, and Filipinos. Defying the rule requiring nonwhites to sit in separate areas, Chavez sat in the larger section reserved for whites and Japanese. When he refused orders to move, he was taken to jail—though he was later released without charges. This was the first time Chavez had openly challenged a rule he believed to be unjust.

> *"I wanted to do more than just be there. I wanted to help. [But] I didn't know anything about unions."*
>
> Cesar Chavez, describing his thoughts as he watched a caravan of striking fruit workers in California in 1948

In 1946, Chavez was honorably discharged from the Navy and returned to his family in Delano, where he went back to work in the fields. Little did he realize that he was about to experience his first taste of a major farm labor strike. In 1948, the San Joaquin Valley Agriculture Labor Bureau set the cotton-picking wage substantially lower than it had been the previous year. The National Farm Labor Union (NFLU), which was already leading a strike for fruit workers in the San Joaquin Valley, called a general strike and set up strike camps in the valley.

A caravan of about 100 cars with loudspeakers drove past Chavez and his family as they were working in a cotton field in Kern County, California. Immediately, the family joined the caravan and hurried to a rally. "I wanted to do more than just be there," he wrote. "I wanted to help. I didn't know anything about unions."[22] He worked in the strike camp, sweeping the headquarters and cleaning the streets during the two weeks that the strike lasted. With the help of the state mediation service, the picking rate was set back to its original $3 per 100 pounds (45 kilograms). This was Chavez's first taste of union victory.

MARRIAGE AND CHILDREN

On Oct. 22, 1948, 21-year-old Chavez married 20-year-old Helen Fabela, whom he had met in a Delano malt shop when he was 15 and she was 14. Born in 1928, she was the pretty daughter of Delano migrant workers from Mexico. She dropped out of high school to help her family. Her father, who fought in the Mexican Revolution (1910), died when she was about 11. She had had a traditional Mexican upbringing, which meant that she was prepared to think always of the benefit of her husband and family before her own.

Cesar and Helen Chavez began their married life in Delano. There, Chavez worked in the vineyards and cotton fields. A year later, Chavez's brother found a job in northern California, and Chavez moved there with his wife to work with a lumber company. The cold, rainy climate was especially harsh on them because they were living in a one-room shack without electricity or running water. The only heat came from a small stove. After little more than a year, Chavez and his wife moved south to the San Jose barrio of Sal Si Puedes.

Chavez and his wife, Helen, pose with six of their eight children in 1968.

In 1949, Fernando, the first of the couple's eight children, was born. He was quickly followed by Sylvia in 1950, Linda in 1951, Eloise in 1952, Anna in 1953, Paul in 1957, Elizabeth in 1958, and Anthony in 1959.

During this time of his early married life, nothing hinted of Chavez's future as a charismatic leader. He was a youthful-looking, unassuming man who stood 5 feet 6 inches (168 centimeters) tall. Slender and quiet, he seemed inconspicuous in a crowd. There was nothing of the machismo of a barrio fighter about him. He "has an Indian's bow nose and lank black hair, with sad eyes and an open smile that is shy and friendly; at moments he is beautiful, like a dark seraph," wrote an observer when Chavez was middle-aged. "There is an effect of being centered in himself so that no energy is wasted, an effect of density; at the same time, he walks as lightly as a fox. One feels immediately that this man does not stumble, and that to get where he is going he will walk all day."[23]

Chapter 2: Education of an Organizer

In 1952, Chavez met two individuals who helped change his life. One of these individuals was an activist priest and the other was a political organizer.

Donald McDonnell, a Roman Catholic priest, had been sent to work in Sal Si Puedes as a result of his own lobbying to create a "mission band" to work with the rural poor. He was sent from San Francisco to minister to the needs of farm laborers called *braceros,* a name that comes from the Spanish word *brazo,* which means *arm.* During World War II, the U.S. Department of Labor used Mexican men as braceros to fill vacant jobs made available in urban factories when Americans were drafted or enlisted into service. These braceros had to agree to work for a set minimum wage and were not granted U.S. citizenship. After the war, they were used by large growers who wanted cheap seasonal labor to harvest fields.

When additional Mexican braceros were brought in to work the U.S. fields after the war, they were not allowed to bring their families with them, and they were hired to work only in certain designated areas. They were prohibited from joining labor unions and were sent back to Mexico if they protested their working or living conditions.

Large numbers of braceros began to be used by large growers in the United States after World War II.

McDonnell initially served as a pastor in camps for braceros and other migrant workers, carrying a portable altar into the field and taking open-air confessions. But it soon became clear that the desperate workers needed something more. McDonnell began teaching the Roman Catholic Church's belief that laborers should join together to work for the common good, hoping to spur interest in organizing the farmworkers for justice.

Chavez and his family attended McDonnell's church in the barrio. According to one story, that was how Chavez met the unusual, youthful priest. But according to another story, Chavez became acquainted with McDonnell when the cleric was knocking on doors in the barrio as part of a survey of Catholics. Whatever the circumstances, Chavez became McDonnell's friend and assistant, helping him with Mass at the migrant camps and the county jail.

They often talked late into the night about the organizing history of labor unions. McDonnell shared important books with Chavez that made a deep impression on him. These included books on labor history, papal encyclicals on labor, the teachings of St. Francis of Assisi, and Louis Fischer's *Life of Mahatma Gandhi*. Chavez became so fascinated by Gandhi that he read everything he could on the Indian independence activist's ideas about nonviolence and sacrifice of oneself for others.

The other key encounter in 1952 for Chavez was with Fred Ross, a native San Franciscan nearly twice Chavez's age. Although he spoke no Spanish, Ross worked in the Sal Si Puedes barrio for community organizer Saul Alinsky's Chicago-based Community Service Organization (CSO) of the Industrial Areas Foundation (IAF). During the early 1940's, the IAF had been established to train community leaders in Chicago's poor neighborhoods to work for social change. After World War II, the IAF focused on Mexican American communities in California. Ross had been sent to Los Angeles to help Mexican Americans register to vote and fight housing discrimination, school segregation, and police brutality.

Ross wanted to expand his work into other areas of California. When he arrived in San Jose, he met with McDonnell to obtain a list of possible community leaders. Cesar Chavez's name was on the list. One afternoon in June 1952, Ross knocked on Chavez's door. Chavez was not at home. Ross left his name and said he would return. At first, Chavez wanted nothing to do with the snooping Anglo, who he assumed must be an academic social scientist or a federal agent. Chavez hid across the street at his brother's house when the stubborn Ross returned again. Helen Chavez was the one who finally convinced her husband to meet Ross. She thought Ross might be able to give Cesar a job.

Chavez decided to set up a meeting with Ross—but with a surprise included. Chavez called some of his toughest friends to his home to have a beer when Ross visited. "I thought we could show this gringo a little bit of how we felt. We'd let him speak a while, and when I gave them the signal, shifting my cigarette from my right hand to the left, we'd tell him off and run him out of the house."[1]

To Chavez's surprise, the tall, lanky Ross seemed sincere. He had described his ideas about ending police brutality and using political clout to improve living conditions for the poor and disadvantaged. Ross impressed Chavez when he told him how the Los Angeles chapter of the CSO had worked to punish eight drunken police officers who had nearly beaten to death seven young Chicanos in a 1951 incident known as "Bloody Christmas." "Never before in the whole history of Los Angeles had any cop ever gotten 'canned' for beating up a Mexican American,"[2] Ross later wrote. Ross and his organization had registered more than 12,000 voters in 1949 and helped catapult the first Mexican American to sit on the city council of Los Angeles since the 1880's. Why couldn't the same changes be made in Sal Si Puedes?

Chavez was so eager to hear more, he forgot to give his friends the cigarette signal. Instead of throwing out his persistent Anglo guest with the big ideas, Chavez had to evict his impatient, tough friends.

Ross explained to Chavez that he was trying to find volunteers to help set up a local CSO chapter. Chavez later recalled: "Fred [Ross] did such a good job of explaining how poor people could build power that I could taste it. I could really feel it. I thought, gee, it's like digging a hole. There's nothing complicated about it."[3]

On another occasion, Chavez reminisced: "I'd never been in a group before, and I didn't know a thing. We were just a bunch of pachucos—you know, long hair and pegged pants. But Fred wanted to get the pachucos involved—no one had really done this—and he knew how to handle the difficulties that came up. He didn't take for granted a lot of little things that other people take for granted when they're working with the poor. He had learned, you know."[4]

Chavez and Ross continued their conversation for several hours. Prophetically, when Ross returned home that evening, he wrote in his diary, "I think I've found the guy I'm looking for."[5]

BECOMING AN ORGANIZER

During the next several months, Chavez became an avid CSO volunteer. "As time went on, Fred [Ross] became sort of my hero," Chavez wrote. "I saw him organize, and I wanted to learn."[6] Ross became not only his hero, he became Chavez's mentor and one of his closest friends.

Chavez got his chance to organize right away. He volunteered to help Ross with a massive CSO voter-registration drive in San Jose for the November 1952 national election. Chavez began as a "bird dog," someone who knocked on doors and asked people to register to vote. Always shy and somewhat self-conscious about his limited grade-school education, Chavez was so nervous when he went to the first house that he forgot what to say.

However, he did not give up. Little by little, his confidence grew. "In about three days I was doing okay," he wrote. "By then it was a challenge. I wouldn't let anybody get away without registering, I'd go into all kinds of arguments, but mostly I'd just sit in the door and not take no for an answer."[7] He developed a kind of little game with himself to beat the other volunteers, who were mostly college students.

He energetically threw himself into his CSO job. Every day after working in the lumber yard, he would return home, eat a quick dinner, and head out into the neighborhoods to knock on doors and encourage people to register to vote.

It was not long before Ross made Chavez chairman of the voter registration drive. Chavez decided not to try to recruit barrio outsiders, such as middle-class college students, to help with voter registration. Instead he convinced 16 of his street-smart friends from Sal Si Puedes to help. Unfortunately, none of them could qualify as a deputy registrar, an official who signs up new voters on the spot. They weren't even eligible to vote, because they had all been convicted of felonies. Even so, they were Chavez's loyal pals, and they diligently knocked on doors to hand out voter registration forms. "They were my friends," Chavez said, "I grew up with them and I knew what they were up against. . . ."[8]

Chavez and his assistants managed to register nearly 6,000 new voters in San Jose. The campaign helped fuel a political fight with the San Jose Republican Party central committee, which was terrified of a political bloc of Mexican American Democrats. The Republicans challenged voters at the polls by making them prove they could read English and were U.S. citizens. Many Mexican American voters were frightened away.

After their election experiences left many Mexican Americans discouraged, Chavez signed a letter to the California attorney general protesting alleged Republican intimidation. Chavez was accused by some Republicans of being a Communist. In the early 1950's, U.S. Senator Joseph McCarthy from Wisconsin hunted down so-called Communist infiltrators in the State Department and U.S. armed forces. McCarthy interviewed suspected radicals on national television and branded them Communists. These accusations, though often unfounded, ruined careers and resulted in deportations. Anyone called a Communist was often publicly persecuted as being anti-American, unpatriotic, and dangerous.

Agents from the Federal Bureau of Investigation (FBI) came to the lumber yard to talk to Chavez and his boss. Chavez was taken by the agents to a meeting with members of the Republican Central Committee. This turned into a shouting match. "That's the first time I started shouting at Anglos, shouting back at them,"[9] Chavez later recalled.

Chavez realized that he had to take action. Toward the end of 1952, a series of unflattering articles appeared in the local newspapers implying that Chavez was a Communist. As a result of this publicity, Chavez discovered that he had support from an unexpected source: liberal San Jose lawyers, social workers, and teachers, who decided to fight the smear campaign. Chavez managed to convince the local priests, with the help of McDonnell, to issue a statement saying that he was not a Communist. This helped convince his neighbors and co-workers, who had been frightened by the accusations against him.

CHANGES IN OUTLOOK

At this point, Chavez began to experience profound changes in his outlook. He was growing and changing from his encounters with people from outside the communities where he lived and worked. His experience of being *red-baited*, or accused of being a Communist, provided him with one of the most painful but powerful lessons about organizing. "When people are fearful, when it's their skin," he said, "they don't care about anybody."[10] Overcoming crippling fear among volunteers and potential union members caused by misinformation, intimidation, and lies would be one of Chavez's ongoing tasks throughout his life as an activist.

Standing up for the rights of others, he discovered, took courage. "My eyes opened, and I paid more attention to political and social events," he said. "I also began to read in a more disciplined way, concentrating at first on . . . biographies of labor organizers like John L. Lewis and Eugene Debs and the Knights of Labor."[11]

When Chavez was laid off from the lumber yard in 1952, just a few months after he met Ross, he began working full-time for the CSO at a starting salary of $35 (about $267 today) per week (later increased to $59 [about $451 today] per week). He helped with voter registration in San Jose and later in Decoto and Oakland, California. "These were hard times in Oakland," Chavez wrote, recalling how some of his friends from the fields ridiculed him as "politico" and "big shot" when they worked for much less than he did. His job was to go out into the tough neighborhoods, talk to residents, and convince them to get together at volunteers' houses for meetings to discuss the area's problems.

Chavez described his first house meeting this way:

I went to the place, but I was so frightened I didn't want to go in, I just kept going around the block. When I got enough courage to stop, I stayed in the car. I couldn't get out of the car. Finally, I went in and found about ten persons there. . . . I just walked in and sat in the corner for about ten, fifteen, maybe twenty minutes. One lady spoke up, "Well it's getting late. I wonder where the organizer is." And I felt I'd die. I just had the strength to say, "Well, I'm the organizer." She looked at me and said, "Umph!" I could tell what she meant, a snotty kid, a kid organizer. . . .[12]

After this experience, Chavez found it easier to arrange and lead house meetings. The hardest part for him was to motivate people to use their own initiative.

LEARNING TO INSPIRE

Chavez gradually learned how to inspire people, how to convince them to take the first step to becoming involved and changing their lives. He learned invaluable lessons on how to listen and watch, how to find out what made different individuals tick. He discovered that he had to spend time with anyone who showed initial interest in getting involved in the organization. "I found that if you work hard enough, you can usually shake people into working too, those who are concerned. You work harder, and they work harder still, up to a point, and then they pass you. Then, of course, they're on their own."[13]

Chavez tirelessly crisscrossed the San Joaquin Valley to set up CSO chapters in several California towns, including Madera, Bakersfield, and Hanford. The plan was to stay in one community for about three or four months and organize before moving to the next. During these early years, he transported his wife and five young children to each new location. His work involved a great deal of sacrifice, including much time away from his family. Chavez admitted that he depended enormously on his partner and wife, Helen, whom he described as "very good . . . too strong to complain."[14]

Migrant workers from Mexico wait in line for work in the United States in the early 1950's.

Organizing was not easy. The CSO was up against harsh racist and antialien opinions in California and throughout the United States. These were difficult, often dangerous times for political organizers who wanted to help powerless Mexican American voters. During the 1950's, about 3.8 million undocumented Mexicans were deported or forced to return to Mexico as a result of an ongoing recession and Operation Wetback, a program created by the U.S. Immigration and Naturalization Service (INS). CSO remained committed to building electoral strength of Mexican Americans through citizenship classes and voter registration efforts.

One of Chavez's jobs was to set up simple, storefront service centers where people from neighborhoods could go for help with such problems as finding lost relatives, locating missing welfare payments, or reading bank loan documents. These centers also offered very practical advice for Mexican American residents who needed to locate a health clinic, find a reputable person to repair a car, or simply discuss a personal problem.

Through this work, Chavez discovered crucial lessons about reciprocity—insights that later would have an enormous impact on his union-organizing style. "Once you helped people," he wrote, "most became very loyal. The people who helped us back when we wanted volunteers were the people we had helped."[15]

Chavez worked with the CSO from 1952 to 1962. By 1962, the CSO organization in California and Arizona would have 22 chapters. Always geared toward working on practical problems—everything from pothole repair to curbing police brutality—the CSO registered thousands of Chicano voters. The CSO also offered citizenship classes and assisted Chicanos with pensions. CSO chapters worked for the installation of sidewalks, paved streets, clinics, and recreational facilities. Slowly, the CSO became an important forum for Mexican Americans' voices to be heard.

ORGANIZING IN OXNARD

During the summer of 1958, Chavez's life took another unexpected turn when he met with Saul Alinsky and other CSO officers to help organize a special CSO chapter in Oxnard, California, a small town north of Los Angeles. Chavez was to help with the United Packinghouse Workers Union in Oxnard. The union served laborers who packed lemons into crates for shipping. For years Chavez had wanted to return to his own roots and organize rural migrant workers. Oxnard was his big chance to help improve working conditions in a place he remembered all too well. It had been in Oxnard many years earlier that his family had spent a cold, wet winter in a tent during a pea and bean harvest.

Chavez began his organizing in Oxnard by devoting many hours to listening to the workers tell their concerns and problems. What he discovered was that local workers were most often turned away from jobs in the fields because growers used braceros during every harvest season. Local workers were paid very poorly as a result.

For an entire year, Chavez and his volunteers sent hundreds of written complaints to the state demanding that locals be hired before braceros. He rallied pickets outside the bracero camps and convinced federal labor investigators to conduct surprise inspections. He staged sit-ins and marches in front of tomato growers and managed to excite the interest of the local media covering the protests. He led a caravan of cars with people singing a marching tune associated with Mexican rebel Pancho Villa (1878–1923) and carrying pictures of the Virgin of Guadaloupe, patron saint of Mexico. The press appeared just at the moment the police arrived.

Chavez speaks to supporters in 1973 about a boycott of grapes called for by the United Farm Workers of America, the union he founded in the 1960's.

In 1959, the growers, who had become weary of bad publicity, gave up and said they would hire locals before braceros. They even offered improved wages: they said workers would now earn 90 cents, instead of the previous 65 cents, per hour. This was a great victory for the CSO, but Chavez soon realized the limitations of their success. The CSO was not in the union-building business. When Chavez moved back to Los Angeles, the workers' movement he had built with such care soon collapsed.

For Chavez, however, the dream of organizing migrant workers remained very much alive. As he explained when he wrote to Ross: "This has been a wonderful experience in Oxnard for me. I never dreamed that so much hell could be raised."[16]

Chavez was promoted in 1959 to executive director of the CSO. In the back of his mind, however, the idea of returning to work with migrant laborers remained. During that year and the next three, he tried to persuade the CSO board to organize farmworkers. No one was interested. The CSO, the board maintained, was a civic organization, not a labor organization.

One of the individuals who encouraged Chavez at the time was Dolores Fernandez Huerta. Shy, unassuming Chavez had met this dynamic CSO organizer from Stockton, California, in 1956 at a CSO fundraiser. He had made so little impression on her at the time that she could hardly remember what he looked like.

DREAMS OF AN INDEPENDENT UNION

By the time the CSO planned its annual convention in the spring of 1962, 35-year-old Chavez had made up his mind to take his work in a new direction. His plan, rooted in his childhood experience on the road and his brief taste of success in Oxnard, was to create an independent farmworkers union. His dream was to persuade growers to sit face-to-face at the bargaining table with the workers who had made them rich. The obstacles, he knew, would be incredible.

Chavez knew from firsthand experience that the majority of workers had no money, spoke little or no English, and often were illiterate in both Spanish and English. Most had no permanent address, making it difficult to mobilize and organize them. Although the workers may have been naturalized citizens, they were treated as outsiders both economically and racially. Farm laborers were often disenfranchised, forgotten, or overlooked by the rest of society.

Any farmworker organization would be up against an extremely powerful, ruthless, organized industry that had succeeded in destroying unionization efforts in California for more than half a century. Chavez was well aware of the failures of union organizers. "It was a sad history of defeat after defeat," Chavez said. "[S]trikes smashed with violence, the government in league with the growers, police helping to bring in scabs [strikebreakers]. But the more I studied the mistakes that were made in the past, the more I believed growers were not invincible."[17]

He remained convinced that Mexican Americans were willing to join unions. As he studied the history of unions in the area, he realized that their failures were often connected to one mistake: attempting to organize and strike at the same time. Patience, he decided, was necessary to build a strong organization before any attempt to challenge corporate growers could be successful. Deep down, Chavez understood that adaptability would be critical.

He persisted in his dream of an independent union. He became more and more convinced that CSO was compromising its radical stance to attract middle-class members:

> *More than anything else I wanted to help farm workers. I was a farm worker when I joined the CSO ten years before, and I thought the organization would help us. . . . I began to realize that a farm work-ers' union was needed to end the exploitation of the workers in the fields, if we were to strike at the roots of their suffering and poverty.*[18]

In 1962, when the CSO refused to back a campaign to organize migrant workers, Chavez boldly quit the only secure job he had ever had. He had eight children, the youngest of whom was only 2 years old. He knew the task he set out to accomplish would be hard both physically and economically. Both his wife and Fred Ross backed his decision.

Soon after leaving CSO, Chavez was offered a job as an organiz-er for the Agricultural Workers Organizing Committee (AWOC), an affiliate of the American Federation of Labor-Congress of Industrial Organizations (AFL-CIO), to organize farmworkers. He turned this down, even though his annual salary would have been about $10,000—more than he had earned with the CSO. He wanted his new union efforts to be independent. Around this same time, he declined another job offer, with an annual salary of $21,000, to work as a director for the U.S. Peace Corps in South America.

When 35-year-old Chavez embarked on his new venture, he had about $1,000 in savings, a battered nine-year-old Mercury station wagon, and a small amount of unemployment insurance payments available—a total budget of about $50 a week for his family of 10. And yet he felt tremendous liberation in making the move, he later recalled. "If you're outraged at conditions, then you can't possibly be free or happy until you devote all your time to changing them and do nothing but that. . . . But you can't change anything if you want to hold onto a good job, a good way of life, and avoid sacrifice."[19]

Chapter 3: The Birth of La Causa

In April 1962, Chavez and his family moved to Delano, the hometown of his brother Richard. Chavez rented a house with a garage; the garage would serve as the organization's headquarters. "I knew no matter what happened," Chavez said, "we always would have a roof over our heads and a place to get a meal."[1] Richard Chavez would prove an invaluable financial supporter in the years ahead. Chavez's sister Rita and her husband also helped keep the union afloat financially, by loaning Chavez money from a mortgage they placed on their house.

Delano had a year-round community of farm laborers. The town was located in the heart of the San Joaquin Valley. From Delano, Chavez canvassed the entire valley and north into the Sacramento Valley, a total area about 550 miles (885 kilometers) long and 80 miles (130 kilometers) wide. In 1960, the state of California had conducted studies showing the dirt-poor reality of its farmworkers. In a survey of 100 field laborers' households in Fresno County, about 25 percent of the households had no way to refrigerate food. Another 25 percent had no indoor plumbing, and less than 50 percent had running water. Many workers lacked regular health care. Approximately half of farmworkers' children under age 18 had never been immunized against poliomyelitis.

Chavez charted this area on a map, targeting 86 towns and labor camps for visits. He drove to each of these locations to distribute questionnaires and talk with poor farmworkers. Day after day, he drove around observing conditions and meeting with workers in their homes. He wanted to find out how much they thought they should be paid. He also wanted to know their opinions about having no Social Security, minimum wage, or unemployment insurance.

THE FARM WORKERS ASSOCIATION

In 1962, Chavez decided initially to name his new organization the Farm Workers Association (FWA) in order to avoid using the term "union," which often frightened workers. Wherever he went, he stressed the service-providing functions of the organization. Systematically, he passed out more than 80,000 questionnaires and talked to thousands of workers. One of the first things he set up was a modest burial-insurance program, as well as a credit union to help members with financial emergencies. These cooperative projects were funded by members. Another cooperative was set up to provide workers with car tires and other automobile supplies at cost. Helen Chavez helped with bookkeeping and eventually became the credit union's administrator.

During these early, lean years of the organization, Chavez logged hundreds of miles and worked 16-hour days. When he could, he took odd jobs as a farm laborer to earn money. His wife went regularly into the fields. She woke up at 4:00 in the morning, fed her children breakfast, prepared lunch, and then left for the fields, where she worked 10-hour days, five days a week, for 85 cents an hour. Every night when she came home, she had to do housekeeping and make dinner. "I think the beginning of the Union was the roughest time we had," said Helen Chavez. "Our kids were very good and very understanding."[2]

She depended on the eldest children, especially Fernando, who was 13 in 1962. Fernando took care of the other children when they were not in school. Because the family could not afford a babysitter, the youngest child, Anthony, often accompanied Chavez on his long drives across the valley. The boy usually slept in the back of the car during the meetings.

Important contacts and assistance for the FWA came from an interdenominational activist church group called California Migrant Ministry. The first week after the Chavez family's arrival in Delano, they met the Reverend Jim Drake, who became a key supporter. Drake was an idealistic Protestant minister with the California Migrant Ministry. Described as an intense young minister, Drake had a passion to reform migrant working conditions, and he quickly became Chavez's traveling administrative assistant. Drake's wife and small child lived in the nearby town of Goshen.

"What impressed me most was that even though Cesar was desperate," Drake remembered, "he didn't want our money, or

Teamster money, or AFL-CIO money, or any other money that might compromise him." Chavez's extraordinary perseverance also amazed the minister. Building the union was a "slow, plodding thing based on hard work and very personal relationships,"[3] Drake said.

The growers never knew when Chavez was in town, but the workers knew. "After a while, they were coming to [Chavez's] house day and night for help." Drake said that word soon went out among the laborers: "If you have trouble, go to Delano. Chavez can help."[4]

Other important early volunteers were Huerta, who was still working with the CSO in Stockton, and Gilbert Padilla, a migrant worker from Hanford, California, who also was active in the CSO. All of these original volunteer staff members sacrificed much—often giving up steady jobs and income—to assist with the early organizing efforts.

EMERGING LEADER

Throughout these early days of FWA house-meetings with members and prospective members, Chavez's leadership style was emerging. His appearance and clothing, his words and language were those of a migrant worker. He had clearly traveled their paths. His identity was obvious. As Blanca Alvarado, vice mayor of San Jose, explained: "[H]is identity as a Chicano, being Mexicano, being Indio, or being part of the ancestry of the people from here was clear, even though he didn't go around banging that drum. He didn't have to tell you that he thought in Indian ways because he acted in an Indian way."[5]

"If you talk to people," Chavez explained, "you're going to organize them. But people aren't going to come to you. You have to go to them. It takes a lot of work." He insisted that the movement had to begin where the people were, where they worked. "The individual is the key to social change," Chavez repeated over and over again to his growing roster of dedicated volunteers. "Nothing changes until the individual changes."[6]

Chavez's willingness to listen, to blend in with a crowd and move with it sometimes perplexed his more impatient staff members, such as Drake. "[Chavez] was the mystical guy who was around, but he was not exerting leadership," Drake once recalled. "[I]t was weird, because things were happening where he was. . . . I still do not really understand it."[7]

Another migrant worker at the time described his first meeting with Chavez while he and other workers were thinning sugar beets with short-handled hoes. "Our first impression of him was that he was interested in us. He wanted to help us, and he listened."[8] Chavez asked about working conditions, sanitary facilities, and wages. Then he passed out questionnaires. In plain speech, Chavez tried to explain the idea of what a union was by comparing it to a cooperative. Chavez found that he had to clearly separate the word "strike" from the word "union," he said, "because in [the workers'] minds those two words were the same. They were frightened of strikes, so I told them this union does not strike, will not strike until we are strong."[9]

> *"The individual is the key to social change. Nothing changes until the individual changes."*
>
> Cesar Chavez

What he envisioned was not a traditional trade union but a social movement—*un movimiento*—that would inspire farmworkers to organize themselves and change their lives.

NATIONAL FARM WORKERS ASSOCIATION

Little by little, the FWA grew. September 30, 1962, was set as the date for an organizing convention to be held in Fresno. Each house meeting was to elect a delegate to present its members' ideas. More than 200 delegates and their families met in an abandoned theater rented for the event. The new official name of the organization was changed to the National Farm Workers Association (NFWA). Union officers were elected. Chavez was named president and executive officer, and Huerta and Padilla were elected vice presidents. The delegates also agreed to set membership dues at $3.50 per month— a lot of money for farm laborers at the time.

During the convention, a huge red banner was unveiled. This was the union's new flag, designed by Chavez's cousin Manuel. The flag featured a black Aztec-style eagle on a white circle. At first the

Chavez leads a group of picketing farmworkers fighting for improved wages and workers' rights in California in 1966.

crowd did not dare to speak. Was the symbol too radical, too dangerous? Manuel Chavez explained how the black eagle symbolized the dark situation of the worker, the white circle represented hope. After this impassioned explanation, the workers voted to accept the flag and adopted the motto, *Viva la Causa* ("Long Live the Cause").

Although he had been elected president, Chavez did not see himself as an administrator. He did not want to be separated from the workers he led. He saw himself as an organizer, leader, and speechmaker. One observer described the way Chavez operated "as father of the Union family, praising, teasing, needling, cajoling, comforting, and gently chastising to maintain balance in this huge and complex household. . . ."[10]

Family was an important theme that Chavez drew upon when he described the union in his early speeches. He was attempting to transform farmworkers from a group of fearful, powerless individuals into a united family that could provide members with services, identity, and influence to change their less-than-ideal lives. "We are a Union family,"[11] he repeated over and over again.

In spite of the success of the September 1962 convention and the members' enthusiastic response to Chavez's message, the first months of the union's life were precarious. It was nearly impossible to keep in touch with dues-paying membership. By December 1962, only a dozen of the original 200-plus delegates from three months earlier were still active. "There were times, of course, when we didn't know whether we'd survive," wrote Chavez. "We'd get members, and then they would drop out. We might go all day collecting dues and then have every single one say, 'I can't pay. I'm sorry, but I don't want to belong any more.' That happened often."[12]

GRASSROOTS ORGANIZING

One way to attract members was to hold free barbecues, Chavez discovered. Hearing about the events by word-of-mouth, migrant farm families would show up, some contributing small amounts against the cost of the food. They then signed up for the union. Not only did these gatherings recruit new members, they also provided a way for Chavez to get the word out about activities and services. One of the most popular vehicles for union news was an underground newspaper that debuted in December 1964 for NFWA members. *El Malcriado* (translated in a number of ways, including "The Unruly One," "The Ill-Bred Child," and "The Spoiled Brat") featured humorous cartoons, irreverent articles, and labor struggle news. Editorials called for living wages and improved safety in the fields.

Meanwhile, Chavez's entire salary continued to come solely from members' contributions, which fluctuated from month to month. He never knew what to count on, but he generally took in about $50 each month—barely enough for his family to survive. Members often shared what food they had to help support Chavez and the other staff volunteers. Humbly asking for food eventually became an important ritual for volunteers who were trying to reach out to prospective members. Chavez admitted that he had trouble with this notion at first. "To me, asking for food was dishonest. I was too caught up with my own . . . false pride," he said. His cousin Manuel taught him the lesson of demonstrating how people are willing to share whatever they had. "From then on, asking for food or for help became another tool in organizing."[13]

It amazed Chavez how the poorest families would often be the most generous with what they had. "[W]e began to find out a lot of beautiful things, how people really are, how the poorer they are, the more open they are, and the more beautiful they are."[14] In spite of a hand-to-mouth existence, Chavez continued to refuse large grants or donations with strings attached. When a private foundation offered in 1963 to give the union $50,000, Chavez turned down the money. He said he wanted the union to rely only on members for its support.

By 1964, the NFWA had attracted 1,000 dues-paying members. More than 50 local chapters had begun in various locations throughout California. Finally, an office for the union was opened in Delano. The office was constructed with labor and supplies donated by members from throughout the San Joaquin Valley. The NFWA, which was still mostly invisible to the public, was growing slowly but steadily.

> *"Nonviolence exacts a very high price from one who practices it. But once you are able to meet that demand then you can do most things, provided you have the time."*
>
> Cesar Chavez

Grassroots organizing required communicating to people their human worth, Chavez said, "and the power they have in numbers." Chavez's years with CSO had taught him that first he and the other volunteers had to isolate a problem that needed to be solved. Then someone had to be willing to solve it, someone "who is willing to take whatever risks are required."[15]

One constant that Chavez came back to again and again in his early speeches to workers and in his private exchanges in houses, fields, and assembly halls was the importance of nonviolence. The concept of nonviolence, which was grounded in his own spirituality, was often difficult for other union members to understand. "Nonviolence exacts a very high price from one who practices it," Chavez admitted. "But once you are able to meet that demand then you can do most things, provided you have the time."[16] He often pointed to the work of Indian peace activist Gandhi, who "showed how a whole nation could be liberated without an army. This is the first time in the history of the world when a huge nation, occupied for over a century, achieved independence by nonviolence. It was a long struggle and it takes time."[17]

IDEAS ABOUT NONVIOLENCE

Chavez was formulating his own ideas about nonviolence during the first years of the NFWA. He constantly reminded union staff and members: "People equate nonviolence with inaction—with not doing anything—and it's not that at all. It's exactly the opposite."[18] Nonviolence, he explained, involved specific tactics that were organized carefully and strategically: picket lines, marches, boycotts, sit-ins, and fasts. Effective nonviolence required mental preparation and carefully following specific rules. Chavez struggled to show members that nonviolence did not mean cowardice. "In some cases," he said, "nonviolence requires more militancy than violence."[19]

Little did Chavez realize how soon circumstances would force him to put his words about nonviolence into practice.

Chapter 4: Union Strikes and Civil Rights

The early- and mid-1960's were a time of tumultuous national change in the United States. It was an era of radical shifts in politics and culture. The presidency of John F. Kennedy, characterized by a youthful idealism, had been cut short in 1963 by an assassin's bullet. While some of Kennedy's New Frontier programs were being slowly absorbed by President Lyndon Johnson's vision of the Great Society and its federal assault on poverty, much remained to be accomplished to create economic and racial equality. African American and white civil rights advocates throughout this period were staging nonviolent boycotts, sit-ins, and marches to demand equal rights for Americans of all races.

WATERSHED YEAR OF 1965

The year 1965 proved to be a watershed. Many people had been filled with hope for a new era of equality after President Johnson signed the Civil Rights Act of 1964, which banned discrimination based on a person's color, race, national origin, religion, or sex. This was one of the nation's strongest civil rights laws. However, 1965 was filled with disappointments for peaceful change. In March of that year, African American leader and civil rights activist Dr. Martin Luther King, Jr., led a nonviolent march from Selma to Montgomery, Alabama, with an estimated 30,000 people to protest that state's refusal to end segregation. During the march, violence broke out and several people were killed. An African American nationalist group known as the Black Muslims rejected King's nonviolent methods and often used force to assert their independence. When their leader, Malcolm X, left the group in 1964, the group accused him of being a traitor. A Black Muslim fatally shot him in New York City on Feb. 21, 1965.

After 11 days of riots in August 1965, the African American neighborhood of Watts in Los Angeles was destroyed, leaving 35 dead, nearly 900 injured, and more than 4,000 arrested. In

Chavez testifies before the U.S. Senate Migrant Labor Subcommittee in March 1966 about his efforts to get California growers to recognize the right of farmworkers to collective bargaining.

November 1965, nearly 35,000 people marched on Washington, D.C., to protest the war in Vietnam. Frustration and civil disorder seemed to be sweeping the land.

For Chavez, the events of 1965 helped catapult his fledgling labor organization into what became *El Movimiento*, a loosely based struggle led by Chicano organizations and individuals—many of them high-school and college students who were committed to ending racist injustice and unfair treatment of migrant workers and to promoting Chicano culture and education. After 1965, the NFWA emerged as "one of many lightning rods for a spirit of protest that swept the land,"[1] according to one historian. Chavez swiftly rose in prominence as one of the best-known Chicano leaders, "a larger-than-life symbol for struggle against exploitation and domination."[2]

Chavez had tried during the NFWA's early years to avoid strikes because he was convinced that the union was not yet strong enough to withstand the full brunt of growers' power. In May 1965, however, he found he had no choice but to strike.

In McFarland, California, workers tended and grafted rose bushes at top speed for several of the biggest flower producers in the country. They had been promised $9 per 1,000 plants but were receiving only between $6.50 and $7. A disgruntled laborer asked Chavez to help him organize a strike. At first Chavez resisted. Then he called together workers for a house meeting. Those present pledged solidarity and agreed to strike the largest company, called Mount Arbor.

Rather than establish a picket line, workers were supposed to refuse to go to work. After several days, strike breakers were brought in from a small town in Mexico. Chavez responded by sending a letter to the town's mayor, who posted it on the town bulletin board. Word spread that these men had betrayed their fellow countrymen. Meanwhile, the company was afraid that its flower crop would spoil if its workers did not return to work. The company agreed to the workers' pay raise, and the workers went back to the fields.

The so-called "War of the Roses" was heralded in *El Malcriado*, even though no contract had been signed. Chavez felt too cautious to celebrate. He believed that the NFWA needed more members to sustain a real victory. Membership growth would take another three years, he said.

Months later, in September 1965, Chavez found that there was no time to wait for the organization to grow as he had planned. The union was thrust into another, bigger strike closer to home. On September 8, in Delano, some 2,000 Filipino workers who were part of the Agricultural Workers Organizing Committee (AWOC) of the American Federation of Labor (AFL) walked off their jobs because they were making less money than braceros. They demanded to receive $1.40 an hour or 25 cents a box for picked grapes. As the strike continued, the AWOC leader went to Chavez for help. Chavez hesitated at first because he was not sure if the workers were ready for a major strike. Finally, he moved to help. He did not want to see the Filipino strike broken.

NFWA leadership scheduled a mass meeting for September 16, which was an emotional and symbolic date for the mostly Mexican American members. September 16 is the anniversary of Mexican Independence. Nearly 6,000 NFWA workers turned out to vote to ratify the NFWA support for the AWOC strike. The turnout amazed Chavez, who made an eloquent speech at Delano's Our Lady of Guadalupe church hall. By comparing the labor battle to the Mexican Revolution fought by his members' ancestors and invoking the spirit of Father Hidalgo—considered the "Father of Mexican Independence"—Chavez cast himself in the powerful image of a revolutionary leader. This strike, which ended up involving more than 5,000 strikers, would last from 1965 until 1970—five years of struggle marked by violence against workers and their supporters.

GALVANIZING SUPPORT

Chavez rose to the challenge of capturing the workers' struggle and putting it into words for a wider audience as he traveled throughout California. He galvanized support for striking workers by going to college campuses. Students eagerly applauded his message that oppressed, maltreated farmworkers deserved fundamental human rights. Television crews trailed him. Footage of police abuse of NFWA picketers ran on nightly news shows. Newspaper and magazine reporters interviewed Chavez, who linked his cause to the expanding awareness about civil rights.

Chavez's quiet, low-key manner made him hard to spot in a crowd. He was no celebrity. Authentic and down-to-earth, Chavez spoke everywhere wearing the clothing of a farmworker. When he spoke he did not swagger. He was soft-spoken but sincere.

For Mexican Americans around the country, Chavez became an important leader. As writer and El Teatro Campesino founder Luis Valdez observed:

> Here was Cesar, burning with a patient fire, poor like us, dark like us, talking quietly, moving people to talk about their problems, attacking the little problems first, and suggesting, always suggesting—never more than that—the solutions that seemed attainable. We didn't know it until we met him, but he was the leader we had been waiting for.[3]

While Mexican Americans embraced Chavez, their long-awaited leader and symbol of hope, others from very different walks of life also found much to admire in him. These included women, other ethnic minorities, and students. "For Chavez, cooperation was the aim of life," one historian wrote. "[C]ommon respect was the basis of cooperation and happiness; and spirituality and humanism were the criteria of respect."[4] As Chavez himself said in a speech: "We must acquaint people with peace—not because capitalism is better or communism is better, but because, as men we are better. . . . We need a cultural revolution. And we need a cultural revolution among ourselves not only in art but also in the realm of the spirit."[5]

In the turbulent, confusing, and often violent times of the 1960's—an era of hatred, militancy, and exclusion—Chavez's message seemed like a breath of fresh air. Here was someone who shunned theories and philosophies. He stood for nonviolent action. While Chavez sought cooperation, he understood the need for power. He wanted society to change, but he knew that social change comes about only when individuals change.

A wide-ranging group gravitated toward Chavez. Many writers described him as an individual who was completely authentic and one whose values came from an earlier era. People were attracted by his common sense and clarity. He had been in the fields. He understood. He was a man of dignity, someone people could trust—an individual with strong personal and family values—who fought against oppression by the rich.

Chavez is shown with his followers in Sacramento on April 11, 1966, after the group completed a 300-mile (480-kilometer) march to gain public and government support for La Causa.

ENCOURAGING NONVIOLENCE

Meanwhile, the reality of organizing and sustaining a five-year strike was often grim and difficult. Growers had developed their own techniques of intimidation, using local police and hired thugs to start fights and harass and degrade picketers. Chavez and his staff had to work hard to use the picket lines as what Chavez called an "educational and recruiting experience." He tried to train strikers to avoid violence as he rallied support from colleges and from Roman Catholic churches around the country. Committed to nonviolence, Chavez drew upon Gandhi's phrase "moral jujitsu" to describe its effect on the opposition. "Always hit the opposition off balance, but keep your principles,"[6] Chavez said. In 1969, he spoke before a union meeting about the importance of nonviolence. "There is no such thing as means and ends. Everything that we do is an end, in itself, that we can never erase. That is why we must make all our actions the kind we would like to be judged on, although they might be our last."[7]

Over and over, Chavez encouraged picketers to maintain nonviolence as a strategy:

If someone commits violence against us, it is much better—if we can—not to react against the violence, but to react in such a way as to get closer to our goal. People don't like to see a nonviolent movement subjected to violence, and there's a lot of support across the country for nonviolence. That's the key point we have going for us.[8]

One of the unique nonviolent outgrowths of the strike was artistic. A radical theater company had been organized in 1965 by the young Luis Valdez after he graduated from college. Valdez, who was from a Delano migrant farm family, founded *El Teatro Campesino* (The Farmworkers Theater), which offered one-act skits performed on the back of flat-bed trucks. These theatrical shows boosted morale and educated and entertained both strikers and workers. The shows were off-beat political satires full of humor that often made fun of the "well-fed boss in sunglasses struggling to learn Spanish so he might enjoy the good life of the Mexican field worker."[9] Wherever there were picket lines, the actors and actresses performed.

During intermissions, musicians led crowds in *De Colores* ("In Colors"), a hymn that became the union's anthem. The joyful song was familiar to many farmworkers as a traditional Mexican folk tune.

Later, El Teatro Campesino would give bilingual performances in cities and barrios and on college campuses to raise money for La Causa. The company toured for several years, offering laughter and insights about economic oppression. In 1967, El Teatro established a cultural center for farmworkers in Del Rey to teach children about their Mexican heritage.

ATTRACTING NATIONAL ATTENTION

While the national media spread Chavez's message, an NBC television documentary, "The Harvest of Shame," helped show viewers what it was like to work and live as a migrant worker.

In December 1965, Chavez asked all Americans to begin boycotting grapes. This boycott aimed to put further pressure on growers to sign contracts and recognize the union. The largest Delano growers were targeted. The boycott's success depended on informed consumers who were sympathetic to the cause.

On March 17, 1966, Chavez organized a 300-mile (480-kilometer) march north from Delano to California's capital, Sacramento, to gain public recognition and secure support for La Causa from California Governor Edmund G. "Pat" Brown. As in the Oxnard march, Chavez made use of many symbols of sacrifice, that are familiar in Mexican American Roman Catholic religious traditions. These were represented by religious statues, banners, songs, prayers, and chants.

Chavez proclaimed that the march would be a *peregrinación* (pilgrimage) to help prepare workers for "the long, long struggle" ahead. The march promoting nonviolence lasted 25 days and ended on Easter Sunday, April 10. Marchers included Filipino, Mexican, and African American members waving all kinds of flags and carrying a statue of the Virgin of Guadalupe. In each town through which the march passed, workers left the fields to join in. Drivers in

Chavez, left, *talks with Wayne C. Hartmire,* right, *director of the California Migrant Ministry, and an unidentified worker in front of union headquarters in Delano in June 1967.*

passing cars honked their horns in support. When the group reached Sacramento, it included about 8,000 marchers and supporters. Although Governor Brown avoided the marchers by going to Palm Springs in southern California, the march received so much national attention that it was deemed a success.

Under pressure from the picketers and the national consumer boycott, representatives from Schenley Industries, one of the large grape growers, and the AWOC and NFWA reached an agreement on April 6, 1966. For the first time in history, a grassroots farm-labor union had obtained what had seemed impossible: recognition by a corporation.

Chapter 5: Struggles with the Teamsters

Following his and the workers' achievement with the grape growers, Chavez immediately began new action. On April 13, 1966, he decided that the union would turn its attention to Di Giorgio, a family-controlled grape-growing company that had vineyards in California and Florida. The company also had thousands of acres of citrus, plum, apricot, and pear orchards. In 1965, the company had netted $231 million. The Di Giorgio operation, which had smashed strikes and unions since 1939, had plenty of experience dealing with union-breaking.

Chavez used boycotts, encouraging consumers not to buy Di Giorgio's products, as a way to convince the large grower to negotiate with workers. Before the boycott was fully underway, Di Giorgio began a deadly cat-and-mouse game. The company appeared to agree to NFWA talks and a union election. But before negotiations could proceed, company guards attacked a picketer. Chavez broke off talks in protest. When Chavez was convinced by Di Giorgio to resume discussions about a union election, he learned that Di Giorgio had invited the Teamsters to recruit NFWA members. Again Chavez canceled talks in protest.

The Teamsters, representing packers and truckers, was a powerful alliance led by Jimmy Hoffa, a corrupt union leader who was alleged to have connections with organized crime. Hundreds of thousands of Teamster members were dependent on agriculture for their livelihood. A boycott or strike of migrant farmworkers would have a negative effect on the trucking industry. To protect its produce-carrying truckers, the national Teamsters decided to create its own farmworkers' organization, which was nothing more than a kind of dupe for the growers.

The secret "sweetheart" deal between the Teamsters and Di Giorgio was simple. The company set up an election among farmworkers, to be held on June 24. The voters were to pick one of four choices: the Teamsters' new union, AWOC, NFWA, or no union at all. This election result would be "fixed" (manipulated in its favor) by the Teamsters. Once the Teamsters' union was selected, a contract that appeared to favor the workers but really favored the company would be handed over to Di Giorgio. The farmworkers would be treated as badly as ever.

Chavez faced an uphill battle against a deceptive, wily adversary. A crooked election, boycotted by NFWA members, prompted Chavez to ask the California governor to investigate. Governor Pat Brown was fighting for his political life in the 1966 gubernatorial election against his Republican challenger, Ronald Reagan. To rally support among Mexican American voters, Governor Brown launched an investigation that resulted in the union election date being delayed until Aug. 30, 1966.

MERGER CREATES UNITED FARM WORKERS

To consolidate power, Chavez made a controversial decision. He and the AWOC's director, William Kircher, agreed to formally merge AWOC and the NFWA to form a new organization called the United Farm Workers Organizing Committee (UFWOC). This name would change again in 1972, when it became the United Farm Workers of America (UFW). Before the August 30 election, Chavez's members voted for the merger, creating the new organization.

Chavez was named director of the new organization. Everything about the original NFWA's goals and strategies would remain the same. The new union, however, would be more broadly based, including Filipino as well as Mexican American members. This inclusiveness, though always part of Chavez's philosophy, was a bitter pill for some individuals who thought La Causa was for Mexican Americans only.

Although some former NFWA and AWOC members left the UFWOC over the Filipino issue and other policy differences, the merger succeeded. UFWOC volunteers attempted to rally every available vote for the August election. Now voters would be asked to choose between only two unions: the Teamsters and the UFWOC. The election resulted in an overwhelming victory for the UFWOC. Dr. King sent Chavez a congratulatory telegram that read: "You and your valiant fellow workers have demonstrated your commitment to righting grievous wrongs forced upon exploited people. We are together with you in spirit and in determination that our dreams for a better tomorrow will be realized."[1]

The battle was not over, however. For the next four years the boycott of Di Giorgio products would continue. Meanwhile, workers on the picket lines continued to be threatened with violence. Chavez had to adjust the union's strategies. Rather than picketing only at the farm entrances, picket lines became mobile and were moved closer to the fields, where workers could be called out and engaged as protesters, too. These roving picket lines reached out to get more participants.

Picketers floated balloons emblazoned with signs that said "Huelga," they sang new songs and chants, and El Teatro Campesino became more popular. Another shift in strategy was that not all growers were harassed simultaneously. Picketing was selective so that workers could continue to find employment in some fields.

Chavez infused the strike with familiar symbols of Mexican American culture and Roman Catholicism. Mass was brought to the picket lines. A mobile chapel was created in the back of a station wagon to help support a round-the-clock vigil. Pilgrimages and marches with flags and statues or posters of the Virgin of Guadalupe were often used as a way of encouraging workers to become publicly committed. Chavez saw the marches of penance as a way to demonstrate the familiar Mexican value of sacrifice.

COUNTERING MILITANCY

In 1968, as the strike and boycott against Di Giorgio began its second year, national events took a violent turn. Race riots erupted in major U.S. cities. Members of the Black Panther Movement, a radical organization founded in 1966, openly favored violent revolution to bring about changes in society. Antiwar protests on college campuses became more violent. An increasingly militant Chicano movement had begun to emerge, with La Causa flags flown at rallies. Some Mexican American leaders were calling for Chicano liberation and nationalism.

On Feb. 15, 1968, to counter the growing sense of militancy, Chavez began a 25-day fast to support nonviolence. This single event—an act of self-sacrifice—attracted much publicity to La Causa. Many volunteers and farmworkers worried that Chavez might die. Concern mounted as people from across the country sympathized with Chavez's nonviolent method of protest. The grape boycott spread.

On March 10, 1968, Robert F. Kennedy, who had long been a supporter of Chavez and the farmworkers, came to California to attend Mass. He broke bread with Chavez, who finally ended the fast. Kennedy, a former U.S. attorney general who would announce his candidacy for the Democratic Party presidential nomination the following week, delivered a speech praising the weakened Chavez. He applauded the sacrifice Chavez had made "against violence, and against lawlessness . . . on behalf of people who suffer so tremendously in this country. . . ."[2]

Chavez's vision expanded dramatically when on March 24, 1968, he announced in Los Angeles a plan for a "worldwide boycott" of California grapes. To build the boycott, Chavez sent volunteers to different cities throughout the country. The volunteers had to raise their own money, find places to live, and recruit local people to help organize the boycott. Some used sit-ins at specific grocery stores that sold boycotted grapes. Other organizers convinced people to write postcards and to telephone store management. A few volunteers created "balloon-ins," releasing balloons inscribed with "Boycott Grapes" inside the stores.

On July 3, 1969, about 80 grape growers and shippers sued Chavez and his union, claiming $25 million in losses because of the boycott. Finally in 1970, after a dramatic and difficult five-year fight, the union won most of its demands. The grape growers signed contracts with UFWOC. As a result, approximately 10,000 union members working for 26 growers were given health insurance benefits, pay raises, and protection against firing. The sweeping victory meant that 85 percent of all table-grape growers in California were under a union contract. Never before had a farmworkers' union achieved such an astounding feat.

Chavez meets with grape pickers in a field in Delano in 1968.

In September 1968, Chavez had suffered from incapacitating back problems and was hospitalized for about three weeks. His ailment turned out to be caused by a pinched nerve in his spine, resulting from a difference in the length of his legs. Beginning in 1969, he received threats against his life and was forced to hire a bodyguard and to use the round-the-clock services of two trained German Shepherd dogs, named Boycott and Huelga.

Violence was stalking other important social and political leaders who were working for peace and justice. A year earlier, on April 4, 1968, Chavez's friend and supporter Martin Luther King, Jr., was assassinated. On June 6, just two months later, Robert F. Kennedy died after an assassin shot him on the night of his victory in the California Democratic presidential primary election. His death was devastating to Chavez and the union.

Nationwide, the poor and the farm-workers had lost two important allies. For many people, the deaths of King and Kennedy created a wide range of emotions, from despair to rage. Many began to wonder how much more violence and bloodshed the country could possibly endure.

MAKE-OR-BREAK STRUGGLE

Almost as soon as the contracts with the grape growers were signed, Chavez and the union became embroiled in one of the biggest, most violent labor confrontations in the United States since the 1930's. This make-or-break situation for the UFWOC was compounded by Teamster violence, intimidation, and dirty tricks.

John Guimarra, seated right, *representing grape growers, meets with Chavez in 1970 to sign a contract ending a long strike against the growers.*

In the summer of 1970, in order to stem the growing tide of support for Chavez and his union, the growers in California's Salinas Valley, called the "Salad Bowl of the World," had secretly united and signed contracts with the Teamsters. The vegetable growers had been terrified by the sweeping success of the grape boycott. To avoid the same fate, they decided on an underhanded tactic. Together they signed contracts with the Teamsters, who claimed they were organizing a new union for about 11,000 farmworkers from Santa Maria north to Salinas. The workers' new terms were not mentioned and would not be revealed until the contracts were signed. In the meantime, according to the Teamster agreement, any laborer who did not endorse the contract or pay Teamster dues would be fired.

When the farmworkers learned about this underhanded ploy, they packed rallies and walked off their jobs. Immediately, Chavez and UFWOC became deeply embroiled in the controversy fueled by the Teamsters' treachery. Teamster thugs were routinely hired to try to break up picket lines. Meanwhile, Chavez began a highly publicized campaign that included a four-day march toward Salinas and a massive national boycott of lettuce.

On Dec. 4, 1970, Chavez was sent to prison on charges of contempt of court. He had been ordered to call off a boycott against a lettuce company, but he boycotted anyway. He was released from prison on December 23, pending the outcome of an appeal.

For the next five years, from 1971 to 1975, the union experienced some of the worst harassment and violence in its history. The undertone of much of the bloodshed was racially motivated: the mostly white Teamsters and growers against members of Chavez's union, who were mostly minority. In 1973, police arrested more than 3,500 farmworkers. A number of UFW picketers were shot or beaten on the picket lines, either by strikebreakers or the police. Two died. These acts of violence were captured by TV camera crews and newspaper photographers.

When many grape growers refused to renew their union contracts in 1973, the grape boycott was initiated again. The farmworkers' movement at this point seemed to be on the verge of destruction. Bitter skirmishes had drained the union reserves. The $1.6 million strike fund from the AFL-CIO had been completely depleted. Union membership had plummeted from about 100,000 in 1972 to only about 5,000 in 1974. Nearly 90 percent of the contracts with grape growers were gone. Instead of 150 contracts, only a dozen remained to cover only 6,500 workers.

The murders of union members while on the picket lines, the bombing of union offices, and the constant threats against Chavez's life created a tremendous weight of guilt, responsibility, and stress. Was the union worth so much sacrifice, so many deaths and injuries?

ALMOST GIVING UP

Richard Chavez, Cesar's brother, who had been involved in the union from the beginning, later said that it was in 1974 that Chavez almost gave up. "He knew we were in very difficult times," Richard said. "Times were going to be very difficult from there on because the opposition was fighting very hard and they would go to any lengths to discourage us from organizing, even as far as killing people." The decision had to be made whether to continue or quit. "We continued," Richard said, "because that's what the people wanted."[3]

During the low point of 1973 and 1974, a new slogan emerged that seemed to sum up so much of what Chavez was struggling to do. The slogan was *Si, Se Puede* ("Yes, it can be done"). The slogan's origin began not in California, but in the most conservative agricultural state, Arizona. Chavez and the UFW decided to become involved in Arizona when a law was created in 1972 to outlaw secondary boycotts and harvest-time strikes. The UFW had tried to fight back against the measure. After the governor of Arizona, Jack Williams, signed the bill into law, the UFW attempted to launch a recall drive against him.

Chavez speaks at a news conference in March 1972 in Miami, Florida, about his agreement with Coca-Cola Foods of Florida on a new contract for citrus harvesters.

In May 1973, Chavez began a fast in Phoenix to rally support and demonstrate his resolve against this antiunion law. Many of Chavez's aides and family were with him in Phoenix. They debated with him whether another fast was a good idea. What would it serve against so many established farmers?

Chavez was repeatedly told that his fast was futile. An Arizona state senator tried to convince him that the campaign against the state law would never work. Over and over, he and labor leaders told Chavez, "*No se puede, no se puede* [It can't be done]." In response Chavez stubbornly replied, "*Si! Si, se puede* [Yes! Yes, it can be done]."

Chavez's fast lasted three-and-a-half weeks. Coretta Scott King, the widow of Martin Luther King, Jr., and other famous individuals

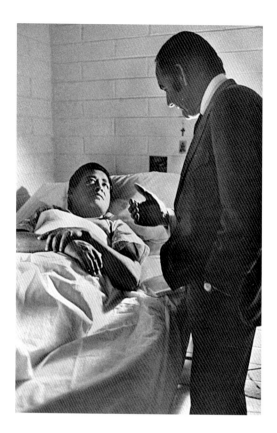

visited him in a show of support. Chavez ended his fast in June 1973; he then attended Mass with about 5,000 people, mostly farmworkers and their families.

The fast inspired a voter-registration campaign with UFW volunteers, who helped register thousands of new voters. Later, these new voters helped elect some of the first Latino and Native American legislators, including Raul H. Castro, Arizona's first Mexican American governor. Unfortunately, the restrictive labor bill was not eliminated.

MARCHING FOR JUSTICE

In 1975, Chavez made a public statement stressing how important it was for farmworkers to get state laws passed that would protect them. On February 22 of that year, Chavez and the UFW decided to march against E. & J. Gallo Winery, which the union had been boycotting since 1973. The aim of the march was to rekindle the old union spirit,

Democratic presidential candidate Senator George McGovern visits with Chavez in May 1973, during one of Chavez's hunger strikes.

bring pressure on Gallo—a Teamster-controlled, formidable agribusiness giant—and raise public awareness in support of giving farmworkers the support and protection of a proposed new farm labor law.

The march began in San Francisco's Union Square with several hundred people. The procession then moved east toward Modesto, California, the Gallo headquarters, 110 miles (176 kilometers) away. By the time the marchers reached Gallo's home office, the group included about 10,000 singing and chanting people. The march helped inspire newly elected California Governor Edmund G. "Jerry" Brown, Jr., the son of former Governor "Pat" Brown, to take the union's demands seriously.

Both the march on Gallo and the lettuce boycott, which ended in 1975, prompted Governor Brown to bring all sides together in support of the California Agricultural Labor Relations Act. On June 5, 1975, Governor Brown signed the act as one of his first political achievements. The act, though difficult to enforce, was designed to guarantee secret-ballot elections for union representatives of farmworkers, allowing the workers to vote without fear of reprisals. The act also sanctioned strikes and created other grievance procedures to handle unfair labor issues. In the ensuing union elections at several major produce companies, the UFW defeated the Teamsters.

The fight against the Teamsters, however, was not over. Chavez soon discovered that the Teamsters were using intimidation tactics in the fields to coerce members into joining their union. On July 1, 1975, the 48-year-old Chavez began a 1,000-mile (1,600-kilometer) march, which would be one of the toughest and least publicized of his nonviolent pilgrimages. His trek started at the Mexico-California border, continued north to Sacramento, and then turned south to La Paz, near Keene, California. La Paz had become the site of UFW headquarters in 1971. He marched when the grape harvest was in full swing. As he walked, he hoped to attract the attention of new members and to speak at rallies.

Notwithstanding the lack of media coverage, Chavez seemed remarkably energetic and revived by the long, difficult pilgrimage though the San Joaquin Valley. A strict vegetarian, he often ate only pieces of watermelon or raw vegetables during the march. Some of his younger staff members recalled having trouble keeping up with him.

Chapter 6: Winning Awards and Settling Old Scores

On Sept. 21, 1973, the UFW held its first constitutional convention in Fresno, California. The 346 delegates, who represented more than 60,000 workers, gathered to hammer out a bill of rights for workers regardless of race or ethnicity. The constitution also attempted to spell out what kinds of direct assistance the union would give to Mexican immigrant workers. No difference was acknowledged between those who were U.S. citizens and those who were not. Chavez's commitment to all people and his union's overarching attempt to be inclusive helped win for Chavez the Martin Luther King, Jr., Nonviolent Peace Prize, which was presented to him by Coretta Scott King in 1974.

Chavez felt especially proud in 1975 when Governor Brown outlawed the use of the short-handled hoe, which had caused so much physical pain to workers in the field and had become a symbol of inhumane treatment of workers. By 1980, Chavez and the UFW were regarded as one of the best-known forces in the Chicano rights movement. More than $1 million had been collected since 1976 from union dues and other contributions to the farmworkers movement. Because of financial stability won after new contracts were made with growers in 1979 as a result of the lettuce strikes, Chavez felt the time was right to push for more lobbying in Sacramento in support of Mexican Americans.

CONTINUING THE STRUGGLE

"The only way is to continue struggling," Chavez explained. "It's just like plateaus. We get a Union, then we want to struggle for something else. . . . After we've got contracts, we have to build more clinics and co-ops, and we've got to resolve the whole question of mechanization. . . . Then there's the whole question of political action. . . . We have to participate in the governing of towns and school boards. We have to make our influence felt everywhere and anywhere."[1]

Chavez had shifted the focus of the UFW to the dangers of pesticides, an issue he had been aware of and had spoken about since the mid-1960's, when he and Dolores Huerta had helped negotiate an end to using such pesticides as DDT and parathion on grape and lettuce crops. That was before U.S. government restrictions on pesticides began in the early 1970's.

Not until the 1980's did Chavez and Huerta's fears appear to be well-founded. Medical research began to indicate a correspondence between powerful pesticides and cases of birth defects and cancer in children of migrant workers. The clusters of young cancer victims showed up in small farmworker communities like Delano in California's San Joaquin Valley. Certain pesticides also began to be linked to illnesses in consumers. Federal government reports revealed that farmers used nearly 2.6 million tons of pesticides each year, and that these chemicals possibly affected the health of 300,000 farmworkers and their family members annually.

In 1984, another boycott of grapes—which would prove to be Chavez's last—was initiated to protest pesticide use. However, the grape growers countered with their own media campaign. Once

Chavez walks alongside Coretta Scott King, widow of Martin Luther King, Jr., during a lettuce boycott march in New York City in 1973.

Protesting the use of chemical pesticides, Chavez calls for one of his many boycotts of grapes at a rally in New York City in 1986.

again Chavez adapted to the challenge. He utilized mass mailings and computerized telephone calling lists to contact supporters directly. When this did not have enough impact, he changed tactics. In June 1988, he began a fast that lasted 36 days to energize the boycott efforts. But the boycott sputtered. In 1989, only a few supermarkets in several California cities supported the UFW boycott.

Chavez and the UFW supported the Immigration Reform and Control Act, passed by Congress in 1986. The act provided, among other things, for the enhancement of border patrols and the granting of *amnesty* (pardon) to certain illegal immigrants. Chavez wanted to protect legal immigrants and make it easier for them to join unions. Although Chavez's position on this issue was essentially pro-Mexican, it alienated certain more radical Chicano groups.

SHIFTING SUPPORT

The supportive audience that Chavez and the UFW had long depended upon was beginning to shift. The union no longer had broad support. American liberalism had changed. Antiwar protesters had grown older. The national mood, once progressive, had become conservative. State and local politics reflected this shift. In 1983, Republican George Deukmejian became governor of California, signaling the end of a sympathetic state government for farmworkers. President Jimmy Carter, a Democrat and labor supporter, had been replaced in the White House in 1981 by conservative Ronald Reagan, the former California governor who had been openly hostile to the UFW.

The decade beginning in 1980 was disastrous for unions, which were slowly being dismantled by businesses and new "deregulation" policies of the U.S. government. By 1990, only one-eighth of the nation's labor force was unionized. The UFW experienced a steep decline in membership. During the last half of the 1980's and early 1990's, the union lost most of its contracts. The media, which had been a long-time ally, now openly criticized Chavez. Segments of the press even blamed Chavez for the UFW's membership and leadership problems.

In 1971, Chavez had moved the union's headquarters from a small piece of land called Forty Acres in Delano, California, to a sprawling former tuberculosis sanitarium at a mountain location that Chavez named La Paz (place of peace). Although the new location offered Chavez plenty of space to conduct agricultural experiments, house union staff, and train volunteers, La Paz was viewed by many members as too isolated from the farmworkers and their concerns. Beginning in the early 1980's, many long-time staff members quit. While some UFW organizers said that Chavez liked delegating authority and enjoyed creating leadership opportunities for promising but inexperienced staff members, others complained that he was a stubborn taskmaster who would not give up overseeing all details of the operation.

PARADOXICAL PERSONALITY

Like Powderly, Chavez was a paradox. He had a strong desire to delegate at the same time he wanted to keep control. Unlike Powderly and the Knights of Labor, however, Chavez designed the UFW to be a centralized organization with no locals. Some staff members, eager to go out into the fields, felt as if Chavez was beginning to lose touch with his members. Others complained that he included too many people from his own large, extended family as union employees. Just as Powderly experienced resistance to strong central leadership, so did Chavez.

Some historians believe that the tremendous moral stature, fame, and authority that Chavez had been laden with by public opinion since 1968 had made it increasingly difficult for him to be approached by less powerful staff members. One of the few people who could approach Chavez, speak openly, and disagree with him was Dolores Huerta.

Being set on a pedestal had its dangers. "In a sense, [his fame] separated him from the other brothers and sisters [in the movement]," wrote Doug Adair, an early staff member and volunteer. "It made it harder for him to really listen, which is what he was best at. And there was no other organizer in the union who was as good an organizer as Cesar. He was the best. He was tops."[2]

ELOQUENT APPEAL

Chavez was never more eloquent than when he spoke on Nov. 9, 1984, before the Commonwealth Club of San Francisco. He had worked hard on his speech, creating many drafts before he was satisfied. Except for convention reports, this would be the first speech he read word for word before a crowd.

The union considered 1984 to be a crisis year, with President Reagan and Governor Deukmejian both viewed as hostile to union interests. At the Commonwealth Club, Chavez was speaking before rich, powerful listeners. He began by telling a shocking true story. "Twenty-one years ago last September," he said, "on a lonely stretch of railroad track paralleling U.S. Highway 101 near Salinas, 32 bracero farmworkers lost their lives in a tragic accident."[3] The vehicle in which they were riding—a flat-bed truck converted into an unlicensed and dangerous bus—was hit by a freight train. All 32 died. No one, not even their employer, knew their names.

Chavez went on to describe how "thousands of farmworkers [still] live under savage conditions—beneath trees and amid garbage and human excrement—near tomato fields in San Diego County."[4] Children, some as young as 6 years old, were being forced to work, he said, pointing to the fact that 30 percent of garlic harvesters in Northern California used underage workers. Nearly 800,000 such children worked in harvests across the United States. Babies born to farmworkers had a 25-percent higher infant mortality rate, a 10-times higher malnutrition rate, and a much lower life expectancy compared with national averages.

Chavez ends a hunger strike in 1988 with the support of his mother and civil rights leader Jesse Jackson.

Chavez illustrated his own experience, how he worked as one of those children. "All my life," he said, "I have been driven by one dream, one goal, one vision: To overthrow a farm-labor system in this nation which treats farm workers as if they were not important human beings."[5]

Chavez related the history of unions in California. He discussed the importance of educating and empowering people and described the UFW's successes. He clearly showed how successes comparable to those in the California fields could happen anywhere—"in the cities, in the courts, in the city councils, in the state legislatures."[6] New union frontiers included ending sexual harassment in the fields and ensuring safe food and healthy working conditions by eliminating dangerous pesticides.

The last point Chavez made was perhaps among his most persuasive. He reminded his audience that south of the Sacramento River in California, "Hispanics constituted more than 25 percent of the population, a figure that would top 30 percent by the year 2000." Chavez was right. The U.S. Census for 2000 reported that

Hispanics comprised between 30 percent and 50 percent of the population in the counties of the San Joaquin Valley. According to Chavez, there were 1.1 million Spanish-surnamed people registered to vote in California in 1984. "We have looked into the future," he told the audience, "and the future is ours!" The day would come "when fair economic and political rewards will accrue, the day will come when politicians do the right thing by our people out of political necessity and not out of charity or idealism."[7]

NOT GIVING UP

By the 1990's, it was clear that UFW boycotts were not attracting attention and support. And yet Chavez did not give up. He kept trying to talk about the power of boycotts and nonviolence whenever he could.

On April 23, 1990, he signed an agreement with the Mexican Social Security Institute allowing Mexican farmworkers in the United States to pay premiums to the institute so their dependents could receive medical benefits from the Mexican government. That same year, on Nov. 12, 1990, President Salinas de Gortari of Mexico awarded Chavez the Aguila Azteca, the highest civilian award in Mexico.

In 1992, Chavez organized a large-scale walkout in California's Coachella Valley during the summer grape harvest to protest the substandard housing conditions and inadequate supply of drinking water for workers. He was able to win concessions from the grower, who allowed the formation of a workers' committee to monitor working conditions. That same year, Chavez rallied walkouts and protests in the San Joaquin and Salinas valleys. In Salinas Valley, 10,000 farmworkers marched for better conditions in the fields.

Moments of success like these helped bolster Chavez's confidence. He remained outspoken about the UFW's ultimate success. "I've been expecting now for years that public support is going to dwindle and disappear, and that we're going to one of these days wake up and find no support there," Chavez wrote. "That's happened to movements. In the last twenty-five years I've seen them come and go very fast, but our Movement hangs on. I think it's struck deep roots."[8]

Chavez was awarded an honorary doctorate degree from Arizona State University in 1992.

RETURN TO YUMA

In April 1993, Chavez traveled to San Luis, Arizona, not far from the small, sun-bleached town where he had been born 66 years earlier. He was there to testify in the union's appeal of a $3-million lawsuit against the UFW that an Arizona court had awarded to Bruce Church Inc., one of the world's largest lettuce producers. In a strange twist of fate, it was this agribusiness giant that had seized the land that the Chavez family lost in 1939 in Yuma, Arizona. Chavez must have recognized the bittersweet irony of returning here—as if to settle an old score.

Church had been a tough UFW adversary for years. If the union's current legal maneuvering failed, the UFW might be forced to pay as much as $3 million to the lettuce giant. With the financially strapped union now reduced to only about 5,000 dues-paying members, it faced the possibility of having its last assets wiped out. How long would the UFW be able to hold on? Chavez was so determined not to allow Church to prevail once again that he began a fast, which he considered a way of gaining "moral strength." Chavez appeared tired after two days on the witness stand. However, his spirit seemed unbowed.

On April 22, following a long day in court, he and another longtime union activist went on a tour of Yuma's working-class barrio. For Chavez, this was a chance to revisit pleasant and unpleasant memories. It was here in this neighborhood, he told his friend, that he and his brother Richard had played stickball. It was also here that his teachers abused him for speaking Spanish.

Chavez broke his fast that evening with a simple meal of cabbage and rice. Relaxed and cheerful, he said goodnight to his hosts and took a book about Native American art to read before he fell asleep.

Chavez never had a chance to finish his last fight against the corporate giant. Some time during the night of April 23, 1993, 66-year-old Chavez died in his sleep of natural causes. It wasn't until three years later, in 1996, that the UFW won its appeal and reached a contract with Bruce Church.

MOURNING AND REMEMBRANCE

Word of Chavez's unexpected death spread quickly in the union field offices and among the field workers. Stunned and saddened, many could not believe that the man who had changed so many lives was gone. Numb with grief, Richard Chavez began to build a plain, pine casket for his brother as he had promised him many years earlier. Chavez had requested a simple burial.

On April 29, a 2.8-mile (4.5-kilometer) funeral procession wound through Delano accompanied by an enormous crowd of about

In April 2003, the U.S. Postal Service honored Cesar Chavez with a postage stamp bearing his likeness. California Governor Gray Davis, second from right of stamp, *joined other area representatives in Los Angeles as the stamp was unveiled.*

35,000 people—mostly ordinary farmworkers, UFW volunteers and organizers of every age, friends, family, and a few celebrities like Ethel Kennedy, the widow of Robert F. Kennedy, former California Governor Jerry Brown, and the Rev. Jesse Jackson.

Some mourners carried stems of white gladiolus, a Mexican symbol of mourning. Others held aloft the red-and-black banners with the UFW thunderbird. The air was filled with *corridos* and *cantos* (songs), and the punctuated chant of *Viva Chavez!* ("Long live Chavez!").

Chavez was buried at Forty Acres, the site of the original UFW field office complex. To summarize his life, his energy, his dream, these powerful words were read during the memorial service: "I am convinced that the truest act of courage, the strongest act of humanity, is to sacrifice ourselves for others in a totally nonviolent struggle for justice. To be human is to suffer for others. God help us to be human."[9] These words, based on something Chavez himself wrote before his first fast in 1968, had become the premise of La Causa.

To honor Chavez's contribution, President Bill Clinton awarded him posthumously the U.S. Medal of Freedom on Aug. 8, 1994. That same year, on September 29, California Governor Pete Wilson signed the Cesar Chavez holiday bill, designating March 21 as a state holiday in Chavez's honor.

A NEW GENERATION

Chavez's struggle goes on, led by new generations of UFW volunteers and organizers. Chavez's son-in-law, Arturo Rodriguez, a union and boycott veteran, became the UFW president in 1993, soon after Chavez's death. Rodriguez's goal has been to revitalize grassroots organizing, while facing continuing threats from increasing economic globalization and conservative governments on national and state levels.

Many problems remain. Long work hours, poor wages, substandard housing, and often nonexistent health care or pensions continue to be facts of life for many farmworkers, whose children attend the worst schools and are exposed to some of the most potent environmental hazards. In the San Joaquin Valley, emissions from pesticides have continued to increase by about 15 percent each year since 1990.

The next generation of UFW volunteers and organizers, following the example of Rodriguez and veteran staff member Dolores Fernandez Huerta, continues the nonviolent struggle for justice for the poor and the oppressed with hard work and their own innovative approaches. Before Fred Ross died in 1993, he spoke of the powerful continuing effect La Causa has had on the labor and social justice movements in the United States. "[M]ake no mistake," Ross said, "La Causa is a force for freedom; and, like all basic struggles of the poor and weak against the rich and powerful, it is geared for a long, long fight."[10]

Pete Velasco, a Filipino immigrant who met Chavez during the 1965 grape strike, summed up the legacy of Chavez and La Causa in a different way. "Cesar was a gift to the farmworkers, to all people, and to me. He taught us how to walk in the jungle and not be afraid. He taught us to maintain dignity."[11] ■

Dolores Huerta (1930–)

Dolores Fernandez Huerta acquired an apt nickname during her years with the United Farm Workers of America (UFW). She became known as Dolores "Huelga," which means "strike." Since 1962, this energetic and fearless UFW leader, lobbyist, and civil rights activist has broken economic and racial barriers not only for farmworkers, the poor, and minority groups, but for women as well.

Huerta worked closely for more than 30 years with Cesar Chavez organizing farmworkers. Since Chavez's death in 1993, she has continued her tireless commitment and involvement as a lobbyist and organizer.

Huerta's story has been largely overshadowed by Chavez's fame, though her importance to him and *La Causa* (The Cause) has been critical. While Chavez was viewed by the media as the highly visible leader, Huerta often worked behind the scenes—out of camera range. "[Chavez] functioned as the catalyst," writes historian Richard Griswold del Castillo, "[Huerta] was the engine."[1] Huerta continues as UFW vice president emeritus and promotes the union agenda as a lobbyist and in various nationwide media outlets.

BACKGROUND AND CHILDHOOD

Dolores Clara Fernandez was born April 10, 1930, in Dawson, New Mexico, a small mining town in the northern part of the state. Nicknamed "Lola," she was the second child and only daughter of Juan and Alicia Chavez Fernandez. Her mother's parents were born in New Mexico, and her father's parents immigrated from Mexico. When she was a toddler, her parents divorced. She moved with her mother and two brothers, first to Las Vegas, New Mexico, then to Stockton, California.

Dolores spent most of her childhood in Stockton. Her neighborhood included many different races: ". . . there was Mexican, Black, White, Indian, Italian," she said, adding "I was a bit luckier than most Chicanos because I was raised in an integrated neighborhood." She did not consider her neighborhood isolated or a "ghetto." "We didn't have a whole bunch of hang-ups," she said, "like hating Anglos, or hating Blacks."[2]

As a single parent, Dolores's mother had a tough time supporting her family. The economic hardships created by the Great Depression, a period of unemployment and financial panic during the 1930's, forced Alicia Fernandez to work two jobs in Stockton. She worked in a cannery at night and as a waitress during the day. Dolores's widowed grandfather, Herculano Chavez, cared for Dolores, her brothers, and, later, their two half sisters.

Dolores enjoyed a close relationship with her grandfather. "[He] kind of raised us . . ." she later remembered. "He was really our father . . . [His] influence was really the male influence in my family."[3] Always feisty, Huerta recalled how her grandfather used to call her *Siete lenguetas* (seven tongues) because she talked so much.

Because her mother worked such long hours, Dolores grew up in a male-dominated household. Even so, she was not expected to do domestic chores such as cooking and laundry for her brothers, younger sisters, and grandfather as most traditional Mexican American girls did. Her upbringing helped shape many of her attitudes about what men and women's jobs should be. "At home, we all shared equally in the household tasks,"[4] she later said.

Her mother's resourcefulness and independence were important influences in her life. "My mother was a strong woman and she did not favor my brothers. There was no idea that men were superior."[5] As she grew older and experienced personal or financial crises, she would turn to her mother again and again for support.

Although Dolores did not have much regular contact with her father when she was young, Juan Fernandez stayed in touch with her as she grew older. As an adult, she looked back with pride on his accomplishments. He worked his way from coal miner and migrant laborer in the beet fields to union activist, working for safer working conditions and better wages. He became secretary treasurer of the Congress of Industrial Organizations (CIO) local at Terrero Camp of American Metals Co. in Las Vegas. After taking college classes, he entered politics. Using his mostly Hispanic local union as his base, he was elected representative for San Miguel County in the New Mexico state legislature in 1938. He worked with other CIO members to promote a labor program that included sections on improving wages and hours. Some historians believe he was not reelected because he was so outspoken and independent.

Dolores would later display the same outspoken and combative tendencies. When she began her own career of union organizing and lobbying, her father was supportive. He was, however, less supportive of her personal lifestyle.

While growing up, Dolores was always encouraged by her mother, who had high expectations for her children. Her middle-class values impressed Dolores, who became active in the Girl Scouts, sang in a church choir, and took dance, violin, and piano lessons. Her mother also reminded Dolores with her own brand of advice: "Be yourself."[6] This would ring true for Huerta years later.

During the 1940's, the family's financial situation improved. Her mother remarried. She and her new husband, James Richards, had a daughter. Dolores did not get along with her stepfather, who eventually divorced her mother. In the early 1950's, her mother married her third husband, Juan Silva, with whom she had a third daughter.

During World War II (1939–1945) and her second marriage, Dolores's mother had begun running a restaurant and hotel for working-class and farmworker clientele. Dolores and her brothers helped with these operations in the summer. Although she described her mother as an ambitious "Mexican-American Horatio Alger type,"[7] she also thought her mother was very generous. Her mother allowed boarders to stay free or pay in onions and other field crops when they were hard up for cash.

Her mother constantly reminded Dolores and her siblings to practice *servicio*, a religious ideal of modest generosity. "You were not supposed to talk about what you did because if you did, then that removed the grace for that good deed,"[8] Huerta said.

EDUCATION, EARLY CAREER, AND MARRIAGES

Dolores attended Lafayette Grammar School and Jackson Junior High School, both in Stockton. Her memories of her early schooling revealed her growing awareness of equality issues. "The teachers treated everybody very mean,"[9] she said. When she went to Stockton High School she became very involved in student clubs. However, she began to notice the very different worlds of the rich and poor. Her high school was very segregated. "There was the real rich and the real poor," she said. "We were poor too, and I got hit with a lot of racial discrimination."[10]

Discrimination raised its ugly head in the classroom, too. When Dolores handed in well-written essays, one of her teachers accused her of plagiarism. How could someone from her background write so well? "That really discouraged me," she later admitted, "because I used to stay up all night and think, and try to make every paper different, and try to put words in there that I thought were nice."[11]

Dolores worked hard because she wanted to go to college. At the same time she could not help but be aware of the poor on the streets. She was sensitive to the fact that the students who had no money were likely to be unpopular or overlooked. Why was life so unfair?

One event that really changed her outlook was a trip she took with her mother to Mexico City when she was about 17. For the first time she was surrounded by Mexicans of all different classes. "[T]hat [trip] opened my eyes," she said, "to that fact that there was nothing wrong with Chicanos."[12] When she returned to the United States she became aware of two realities: societal injustices and her own lack of activism. She decided she needed to do something.

Always a gregarious person, she had a flare for organizing groups of fellow students. A former classmate recalled how Dolores was very popular and outspoken. Unlike most Hispanic women of her generation, however, she continued her education at Stockton College (now San Joaquin Delta College). "I felt I had all of these frustrations inside of me," she said. "I had a fantastic complex because I seemed to be out of step with everybody and everything. You're trying to go to school and yet you see all of these injustices. It was just such a complex!"[13]

In 1950, when she was 20, she married her high school sweetheart. She and Ralph Head had two daughters. Within just a few years, they were divorced.

Dolores became active in Hispanic women's groups, such as the Comité Honor'fico Women's Club, attempting to follow the traditional elite Mexican woman's activist role: to serve in all-women organizations. However, she discovered that this kind of civic virtue—that "didn't do anything but give dances and celebrate the Fiestas Patrias [patriotic holidays]"[14]—failed to satisfy her.

As a single mother, Dolores worked at a variety of jobs in Stockton, including managing her mother's neighborhood grocery store and doing clerical work in the sheriff's office. When she felt she had hit a dead end with jobs, she decided to go back to Stockton College. There, she obtained a provisional teacher's certificate, which allowed her to work in the classroom. This, too, proved unsatisfying. She taught for only a short time. "I realized one day that as teacher I couldn't do anything for the kids who came to school barefoot and hungry,"[15] she said.

> *"I realized one day that as teacher I couldn't do anything for the kids who came to school barefoot and hungry."*
>
> Dolores Huerta, speaking of her dissatisfaction with her teaching experiences of the 1950's

Around 1955, she married Ventura Huerta, a health administrator and community activist with whom she would have five children. They had a difficult marriage because of disagreements about her growing community activist career. She later said: "I knew I wasn't comfortable in a wife's role, but I wasn't clearly facing the issue. I hedged, I made excuses, I didn't come out and tell my husband that I cared more about helping other people than cleaning my house and doing my hair."[16] During a trial separation and eventual divorce, Dolores depended on her mother for economic help, baby-sitting assistance, and moral support as she performed her community work.

COMMUNITY ORGANIZING

In 1955, the year she was balancing her divorce from Ventura Huerta, the care of seven small children, and the completion of her community college degree, Huerta met someone who would change her life. Fred Ross, who had also had a profound influence on Cesar Chavez, was the individual who tapped into Huerta's growing awareness that she could change her life and, perhaps, the lives of other people.

A new wave of civic activism was beginning to emerge in Mexican American communities, including Stockton's *barrios* (neighborhoods). One of the new initiatives was the Community Service Organization (CSO), a Mexican American self-help association based in Los Angeles that began as part of community organizer Saul Alinsky's Industrial Areas Foundation in Chicago. CSO's voter registration efforts had been crucial in helping to elect Edward Roybal, the first Hispanic member of the Los Angeles City Council, in 1949. Huerta was captivated by Saul Alinsky's pragmatic message. She liked the idea that it was the poor who achieved reform for themselves.

At first, Fred Ross, chief organizer of the CSO, made Huerta suspicious. "I thought he was a communist,"[17] she admitted. Such a belief was the result of her dyed-in-the wool middle-class outlook at the time. She even had Ross investigated by the Federal Bureau of Investigation (FBI)—an action that she later found embarrassing.

As soon as she realized that her assumption about Ross was wrong, she became active in helping neighbors register to vote, organizing citizenship classes, and demanding improvements in the barrio. Like the 19th-century American labor leader Terence Powderly, she found personal fulfillment in her job as an organizer.

In time she became so bold, aggressive, and successful at persuading people that she was hired by the CSO as a lobbyist in Sacramento, California's capital, where she pushed such CSO legislative initiatives as providing old-age pensions for legal immigrants. "I think women are particularly good negotiators and organizers because we have a lot of patience," she later said, "and no ego trips to overcome."[18]

Her first meeting with Chavez came in 1956 through their mutual involvement in CSO. She recalled seeing him again at a CSO board meeting in Stockton in July 1958. Each of the chapters had sent delegates to the meeting, and Huerta represented the Stockton chapter. She had heard a great deal from Ross about what a superb organizer Chavez was. "Cesar was very quiet, very unassuming in every meeting," she said. "I mean he never spoke up, although he was an organizer like Fred was. So he was kind of a hard guy to know."[19]

When Chavez finally did speak during a particularly tumultuous argument, however, he made a big impression on her. "I can't remember exactly all the things he said, but he impressed me very much because of the soft-spoken, very gentle way that he had about him in presenting what he thought was his situation. It was kind of like a lamb in the midst of a bunch of lions."[20]

Chavez and Huerta would soon discover a mutual interest in working for the welfare of farmworkers. Meanwhile, in 1958 Huerta found a way to help migrant laborers with the help of Thomas McCullough, a Roman Catholic priest in Stockton. McCullough wanted to set up a new group called the Agricultural Workers Association (AWA). He had complained that farmworkers had been abandoned by the American Federation of Labor-Congress of Industrial Organizations (AFL-CIO). Although McCullough told Huerta that "organizing farmworkers was not the kind of work a woman should be doing," she became involved in the AWA effort. Within a year, the AWA received funding from the AFL-CIO and was transformed in 1959 into the Agricultural Workers Organizing Committee (AWOC). Disregarding McCullough's advice, Huerta served as the AWOC's secretary-treasurer.

The idea behind the AWOC was to organize Filipino and other minority farm laborers in California. Unfortunately, the AWOC seemed unable to reach out to Mexican American farmworkers. Most of the AWOC officials were white, spoke no Spanish, and had no direct experience in the fields. Huerta was frustrated because the union officials seldom left the office. In 1960, she

> *". . . he impressed me very much because of the soft-spoken, very gentle way that he had about him. . . . It was kind of like a lamb in the midst of a bunch of lions."*
>
> Dolores Huerta, speaking of her early impressions of Cesar Chavez

decided to leave the AWOC, though she remained on good terms with the organization.

For the next two years, from 1960 to 1962, she worked part-time as a lobbyist for the CSO in Sacramento—in what was often a hostile environment. In 1960, she was the only woman to testify before a California Senate committee hearing on labor and welfare. At the hearing, she spoke out against the mistreatment of farmworkers.

In Sacramento, she worked hard to lobby for legislation that helped remove the citizenship requirement for people trying to obtain pensions. She focused her energy on public assistance programs for Mexican Americans, trying to convince lawmakers to give non-English speakers the right to take the driver's license examination in the their native language.

In 1962, Huerta lobbied in Washington, D.C., to end the "captive labor" of the *bracero* (day laborer) program. Under this program, Mexican day laborers could enter the United States legally for seasonal agricultural work and for work on U.S. railroads. These braceros often worked under harsh conditions for unsympathetic employers, but they accepted the work because they were unable to find jobs in Mexico.

KEY ROLE IN THE FARM WORKERS ASSOCIATION

Despite the contacts she had developed in Sacramento and Washington, D.C., and her growing involvement in labor issues, Huerta had no plans for leaving the CSO. However, when Chavez suddenly left the CSO in 1962 to begin an independent farmworkers union, she realized how committed she was to his vision. In an undated letter to Chavez, Huerta wrote about her enthusiasm for the new farmworkers union: "We have a hell of a task in front of us, but I do not think the task is impossible."[21]

Although Huerta had been involved with the union since its inception, her role didn't become official until she was voted first vice president at the union's inaugural convention in September 1962. Also at this convention, the official name of the union was adopted: the National Farm Workers Association (NFWA). Huerta soon discovered that some of the male farmworkers and union organizers found her presence upsetting. Some refused to talk to her during meetings. Others made sexist jokes or remarks. Even some of her friends counseled against what she was doing. "People thought I was a little loony because I was . . . going through a [second] divorce and I had seven children and was going to quit my job teaching to come organize the union."[22]

In spite of negative feedback, she was determined to follow her dream. Somehow she felt she could keep her family afloat even though they would have to live on meager unemployment insurance and child-support checks from her two ex-husbands. Like Chavez and his family, Huerta made tremendous financial and personal sacrifices for the new union. Yet she was also honest about her anxiety about the future. "I am not the quiet, long-suffering type," she told Chavez in a letter. She reminded him that she needed money to pay for gas and she might also need to use his car to help him. "If I can make it through August," she wrote in another letter to Chavez, "and I know the Good Lord will not let us starve, then in September I can apply for my substitute teacher credential."[23]

Huerta remained in Stockton until 1964, when she pulled up stakes, packed up her seven children and few worldly belongings, and moved to Delano, California, where the home office of the NFWA was located. She had $30 a week to live on, plus child-support checks and whatever extra food union volunteers might donate. The day she made the decision to move, she recalled, someone left a big box of groceries on her porch in

Chavez speaks with Huerta at NFWA headquarters in Delano, California, during a 1968 grape pickers strike.

Stockton. She took this as a kind of sign. "It was a very, very hard time for us," she later recalled. At the time she felt very sad and guilty about sending her children to school in shoes with holes. And yet she reminded herself, "[T]his is what farmworker families go through every day of their lives."[24]

Her first big organizing effort came during the Delano grape strike in September 1965, when more than 5,000 workers walked off the job. She was instrumental in merging two very different organizations, the NFWA and the AWOC, into a new union called the United Farm Workers Organizing Committee (UFWOC). In 1972, the union changed its name to the United Farm Workers of America (UFW).

Huerta's selfless leadership and organizing talents were described by artist Luis Valdez, producer of *El Teatro Campesino* (The Farmworkers' Theater): "Dolores was a 35-year-old firebrand in 1965, and she was commanding crusty macho *campesinos* [agricultural workers] 20 years her senior. What dazzled my radicalized university-trained Chicano mind was that she led through persuasion and personal example, rather than intimidation, and that she was one hell of an organizer. People tend to forget that the 1960's were the sexist dark ages, even in the Chicano movement, as we called it, but Dolores was already way out in front. She was a woman, a Mexican American, a Chicana cutting a swath of revolutionary action across the torpidity of the San Joaquin Valley."[25]

"The whole thrust of our boycott is to get as many supporters involved as you can."

Dolores Huerta, describing her work of organizing union volunteers during the late 1960's

She remained convinced that the energy and equal participation of women was very important in building the union, noting, "The participation of women has helped keep the movement nonviolent."[26] She frequently claimed that women were more patient and less volatile than men. Although she could be tough, patience would serve her well during difficult negotiations.

In 1966, Huerta was thrust into another unexpected, high-stakes role as the first UFWOC negotiator during a strike. It was around this time that she acquired her new nickname, "Huelga." She had not been trained as a lawyer and had no negotiating experience. She had never read a labor contract before the strike began, yet she found herself in the role of negotiator. She used an unorthodox, often forceful style face-to-face with powerful growers. "Dolores Huerta is crazy," complained one agribusiness executive in a *Progressive* interview in 1975. "She's a violent woman, where women, especially Mexican women, are usually peaceful and pleasant."[27]

Huerta soon gained a reputation as a stubborn, passionate feminist in the backroom politicking environment of union negotiating, traditionally a man's world. To her credit, she negotiated the first hard-won UFWOC contract with Schenley Wine Co. Discussions and meetings would often be held nonstop. In 1967, when she negotiated contracts for workers with Almaden Vineyards, she and two other union staffers did not complete their discussions until 4:00 in the morning in San Francisco. She described these marathon sessions as sometimes "painful."[28] After not sleeping for two days during the completion of the Almaden deal, she was so exhausted that she fainted and ended up in the hospital. After resting in bed for three days, she headed back to the fields again.

ORGANIZING BOYCOTTS AND STRIKES

In 1968 and 1969, Huerta shifted gears from her role as arbitrator and went to New York City to act as East Coast coordinator for the table grape boycott. Her job was to organize volunteers and set up picket lines in such places as terminal markets, the large loading points for produce. She worked to attract volunteers, from peace activists, community organizers, and student protesters, to Hispanic activists, consumers, and religious supporters. "The whole thrust of our boycott is to get as many supporters involved as you can,"[29] she explained to an interviewer during this period. The grape boycott's grassroots coalition across the nation remained active for five years. Its success helped draw grape producers in Coachella and Delano, California, to the negotiating table.

Huerta's experiences in New York had important effects on her outlook. She became more aware of the feminist movement, meeting with activist Gloria Steinem. These experiences changed much of the content of her speeches from this point onward. The goal of communicating with a larger audience of both men and women would be advanced several years later when she helped found another ambitious project, a union radio station called KUFW-Radio Campesina. The station would become part of the National Farm Workers Service Center in the 1980's.

Deeply aware of the impact of the use of pesticides on children, she became an outspoken critic of pesticide use in the late 1960's. She was especially critical of the use of DDT and parathion.

During the 1968 presidential primary, she and other Chicana volunteers and UFWOC members worked diligently in California to register voters and rally support for Robert F. Kennedy, who was campaigning for the Democratic presidential nomination in the California primary election. Huerta took the stage with Kennedy and many other supporters on June 5, 1968, during his victory party on primary election night at the Ambassador Hotel in Los Angeles. Kennedy thanked Huerta and Chavez for their help rallying Mexican American voters. Then he uttered his last public words: "On to Chicago, and let's win there!"

In the crush of well-wishers, Huerta was separated from Kennedy, who was ushered off the platform. He made his way through an exit from the ballroom into the kitchen, where he was shot by assassin Sirhan Sirhan. Kennedy died the next day. Like so many other supporters, Huerta was deeply affected by Kennedy's death.

The pressure of organizing boycotts resumed in the 1970's, when Huerta returned to New York to help spearhead volunteer organizing for the lettuce, grape, and Gallo wine boycotts. As a result of the success of these efforts, workers were finally given contracts. She was instrumental in helping set up hiring halls and *ranch committees,* small groups of farmworkers who represent all workers on a ranch in negotiations with the owner. In so doing, she helped reduce the power of unscrupulous farm labor contractors. She assisted in conducting more than 100 grievance procedures on behalf of workers. After California Governor Edmund G. "Jerry"

Brown, Jr., signed the California Agricultural Labor Relations Act in 1975, Huerta focused her lobbying efforts in Sacramento on the legislative arm of UFWOC dedicated to protecting the rights of workers.

PERSONAL AND FAMILY SACRIFICES

At about 5 feet 1 inch (155 centimeters) tall, Huerta is a small woman. For most of her life, she has had long, dark hair. One observer described her as "slender, with striking Indian features. . . . Her tongue moved as swiftly as her mind, and both left most other mortals in their wake." Her almost superhuman stamina has always been remarkable, according to observers. "I imagine that if I had known [activist] Emma Goldman, she would have been something like Dolores," feminist activist Gloria Steinem said in an interview after she had known Huerta for almost 30 years. "She's not a person whose life is divided into public and private, work and play—it's all of a piece."[30]

Throughout her career, Huerta often took her children with her to the picket lines and union meetings. Often she moved her children when she had to relocate to Los Angeles, New York, or Chicago for union work. The hectic activity of boycott organizing, contract arbitration, and lobbying during the 1970's created an especially demanding traveling and speaking schedule. During this time she began a long-distance relationship with Richard Chavez, the brother of Cesar Chavez. Together they had four children. When her first child was born, she was 20; her last and 11th child was born when she was 46. Her large number of children is the result, she says, of her respect for the tenets of the Roman Catholic Church, which opposes artificial birth control.

> *"She's not a person whose life is divided into public and private, work and play—it's all of a piece."*
>
> Feminist activist Gloria Steinem, referring to Huerta in a 1998 interview

Throughout her union career, Huerta was frequently absent from her home and children. As a result, she often had to endure criticism of neglect of her family from both farmworking women and middle-class volunteers. "I don't feel proud of the suffering that my kids went through," she once said in an interview. "I feel very bad and guilty about it, but by the same token I know that they learned a lot in the process."[31]

Her 45-year-old daughter Lori admitted in a 1998 interview that the union always came first for her mother. "I remember, as a child, one time talking to her about my sadness that she wasn't going to be with me on my birthday. And she said that the sacrifices we as her children make would help hundreds of other children in the future. How can you argue with something like that?"[32]

Another of Huerta's daughters, 26-year-old Juanita, told the interviewer in 1998 that her mother is without question her hero. "But what I love about my hero is that she doesn't try to be perfect. She will be the first to admit her faults."[33]

Huerta's commitment to the union has come at great personal cost. Over the years, her fearlessness in the face of police intimidation and threats became legendary. In the course of her organizing efforts, she has been arrested more than 20 times during peaceful protests. Her FBI record goes back to the 1960's, when she was first extensively investigated. In one FBI report she was paid a backhanded compliment when she was described as "the driving force on the picket lines of Delano and Tulare County."[34]

Undoubtedly one of the most dangerous physical confrontations for Huerta came in September 1988, during a peaceful demonstration against the policies of then presidential candidate George H. W. Bush. Bush was campaigning in San Francisco.

When violence broke out, baton-swinging police officers attacked Huerta. A 6-foot 7-inch (200-centimeter) officer

Huerta attended a symposium honoring the late Robert F. Kennedy at Loyola Marymount University in Westchester, Connecticut, in 1989.

clubbed her in the back, broke some of her ribs, and destroyed her spleen. She was rushed to the hospital, where she underwent emergency surgery to have her spleen removed. The incident and her ensuing lawsuit against the police caused the San Francisco police department to change its rules regarding crowd control. Huerta won a sizable financial settlement as a result of the personal assault.

After two years of recuperation, she gradually returned to her work with the UFW in 1990. The following year she became active in the Feminist Majority's Feminization of Power campaign, a project that encourages Hispanic American women to run for public office.

After Cesar Chavez's unexpected death in 1993, Huerta continued to foster UFW work in the political arena and on labor issues. Her work was recognized with several awards she received in 1993, included induction into the National Women's Hall of Fame. Also in 1993, she was awarded the Roger N. Baldwin Medal of Liberty from the American Civil Liberties Union, the Eugene V. Debs Foundation Award, and the Ellis Island Medal of Honor.

In 1996, she began organizing some 20,000 strawberry workers in the Salinas Valley of California. She took time off from union work in 1999 to help U.S. Vice President Al Gore's presidential campaign. In 2000, she again had to take time out from her union work, this time to be hospitalized because of an ulcer.

Presented with the 1999 Eleanor Roosevelt Human Rights Award by U.S. President Bill Clinton and the prestigious 2000 Hispanic Heritage Award, Huerta remains indefatigable into the 2000's. She has been committed to fighting sexual harassment and improving working conditions in the fields. She continues to support La Causa and women's rights on a number of fronts, including serving as vice president of the Coalition of Labor Union Women. Many challenges remain ahead for the UFW, according to Huerta.

In spite of many setbacks, Huerta feels confident that the kind of nonviolence and political action that the UFW has as its cornerstone will succeed in the end to help create justice for the poor, minorities, and women. She remains intensely proud of the UFW's accomplishments. "I think we brought to the world, the United States anyway, the whole idea of boycotting as a nonviolent tactic. I think we showed the world that nonviolence can work to make social change. . . . I think we have laid a pattern of how farm workers are eventually going to get out of their bondage. It may not happen right now in our foreseeable future, but the pattern is there and farm workers are going to make it."[35] ■

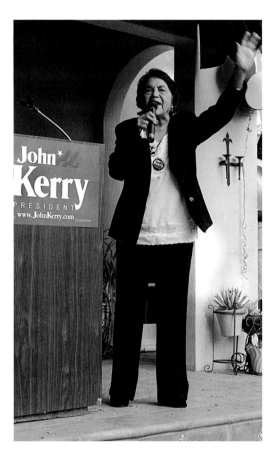

Huerta campaigns for Democratic presidential candidate Senator John F. Kerry of Massachusetts in 2004. Kerry lost the election to President George W. Bush.

Notes

PREFACE

1. Richard Griswold del Castillo and Richard A. Garcia, *César Chávez: A Triumph of Spirit* (Norman, OK: University of Oklahoma Press, 1995) 75.

TERENCE V. POWDERLY

1. Terence Vincent Powderly, "The Army of the Discontented," *North American Review* April 1885: 369-377, qtd. in Craig Phelan, *Grand Master Workman: Terence Powderly and the Knights of Labor* (Westport, CT: Greenwood Press, 2000) 3.
2. Phelan 3.
3. Terence Vincent Powderly, *The Path I Trod.* 1940 (New York: AMS Press, 1968) 14.
4. Powderly, *The Path I Trod* 14.
5. Powderly, *The Path I Trod* 11.
6. Powderly, *The Path I Trod* 278.
7. Terence Vincent Powderly Diary, end 1879; Jan. 24, 1869; Feb. 2, 1870, qtd. in Phelan 15.
8. Powderly, *The Path I Trod* viii.
9. Robert E. Weir, *Beyond Labor's Veil: The Culture of the Knights of Labor* (University Park, PA: The Pennsylvania State University Press, 1996) 10.
10. Qtd. in Weir 46.
11. Qtd. in Phelan 47.
12. *John Swinton's Paper* 17 Oct. 1886, qtd. in Powderly, *The Path I Trod* viii-ix.
13. Phelan 48, 56.
14. Phelan 64.
15. Phelan 129.
16. Knights of Labor, *Proceedings of the General Assembly, 1885* 7-8, qtd. in Phelan 150.
17. Phelan 153.
18. *Scranton Truth* 6 Feb. 1885, qtd. in Phelan 153.
19. Phelan 153.
20. Powderly, *The Path I Trod* xi.
21. *Wheeling Register* 9 May 1882; *Proceedings of the General Assembly, 1880* 170, qtd. in Phelan 57.
22. *Journal of United Labor* February 1883, qtd. in Phelan 59.
23. Weir 12.
24. Terence Vincent Powderly, *Thirty Years of Labor* (Columbus, OH: Excelsior Pub. House, 1889) 6.
25. Powderly, *The Path I Trod* vii.
26. Qtd. in Phelan 261.
27. Mary Harris Jones, *The Autobiography of Mother Jones* 3rd ed., rev. (Chicago: Charles H. Kerr, 1976) 14.

CESAR CHAVEZ

Chapter 1

1. Jacques E Levy, *Cesar Chavez: Autobiography of La Causa* (New York: W. W. Norton & Co. Inc., 1975) 17.
2. Levy 8.
3. Levy 18.
4. Levy 19.
5. Levy 27.
6. Levy 36-37.
7. Levy 37.
8. Susan Ferriss and Ricardo Sandoval, *The Fight in the Fields: Cesar Chavez and the Farmworkers Movement* (New York: HarcourtBrace, 1997) 17.
9. Qtd. in Ferriss 19.
10. Levy 48.
11. Qtd. in Ferriss 18.
12. Levy 74.
13. Levy 58-59.
14. Qtd. in Ronald B. Taylor, *Chavez and The Farm Workers* (Boston: Beacon Press, 1975) 62.
15. Qtd. in Ferriss 26.
16. Levy 65.
17. Levy 78.
18. Qtd. in Ferriss 23.
19. Qtd. in Taylor 63.
20. Qtd. in Ferriss 33.
21. Levy 84.
22. Qtd. in Taylor 70.
23. Qtd. in Peter Matthiessen, *Sal Si Puedes: Cesar Chavez and the New American Revolution* (New York: Random House, 1973) 6.

Chapter 2

1. Levy 98.
2. Qtd. in Ferriss 42.
3. Levy 99.
4. Qtd. in Ferriss 43.
5. Levy 102.
6. Levy 99.
7. Levy 104.
8. Qtd. in Ferriss 45.
9. Levy 106.
10. Levy 118.
11. Levy 108.
12. Levy 113.
13. Qtd. in John Gregory Dunne, *Delano*, rev. (New York: Farrar Strauss & Giroux, 1971) 69-70.
14. Levy 114.
15. Levy 111.
16. Qtd. in Ferriss 60.
17. Levy 4.
18. Levy 3.
19. Qtd. in John C. Hammerback and Richard J. Jensen, *The Rhetorical Career of Cesar Chavez* (College Station, TX: Texas A&M University Press, 1998) 21.

Chapter 3

1. Levy 157.
2. Levy 159.
3. Levy 162.
4. Levy 162.
5. Qtd. in Hammerback 26.
6. Qtd. in Hammerback 27.
7. Qtd. in Taylor 113-114.
8. Qtd. in Taylor 114.
9. Qtd. in Taylor 114.
10. Matthiessen 116.
11. Qtd. in Hammerback 29.
12. Levy 178.
13. Levy 166, 167.
14. Levy 163.
15. Qtd. in Hammerback 33.
16. Qtd. in Hammerback 35.
17. Qtd. in Hammerback 35.
18. Levy 269.
19. Qtd. in Hammerback 37.

Chapter 4

1. Richard Griswold del Castillo and Richard A. Garcia, *César Chávez: A Triumph of Spirit* (Norman, OK: University of Oklahoma Press, 1995) 42.
2. Griswold del Castillo 42.
3. Luis Valdez, "The Tale of La Raza," *The Chicanos: Mexican-American Voices* 96, qtd. in Hammerback 76.
4. Qtd. in Griswold del Castillo 98.
5. Qtd. in Griswold del Castillo 98.
6. Qtd. in Griswold del Castillo 270.
7. Qtd. in Griswold del Castillo 47.
8. Levy 195-196.
9. Ferriss 111.

Chapter 5

1. Qtd. in Levy 246.
2. "César Chávez Stories," ABC News, Reel 210, 1968, qtd. in Hammerback 73.
3. Ferriss 188.

Chapter 6

1. Levy 536-537.
2. Qtd. in Ferriss 225.
3. Qtd. in Hammerback 161.
4. Hammerback 161-162.
5. Qtd. in Hammerback 162.
6. Qtd. in Hammerback 163.
7. Hammerback 165, 166.
8. Levy 517.
9. Levy 286.
10. Qtd. in Levy xxv.
11. Qtd. in Ferriss 268.

DOLORES HUERTA

1. Richard Griswold del Castillo and Richard A. Garcia, *Cesar Chavez: A Triumph of Spirit* (Norman, OK: University of Oklahoma Press, 1995) 59.
2. Dolores Huerta, "Un Soldado del Movimiento," *With These Hands: Working Women on the Land,* Joan M. Jensen (Old Westbury, NY: The Feminist Press, 1981) 216.
3. Qtd. in Margaret Rose, "Dolores Huerta," *Dictionary of Hispanic Biography* (Detroit: Gale Research, 1996) 435.
4. Qtd. in Griswold del Castillo 62.
5. Qtd. in Griswold del Castillo 64.
6. Griswold del Castillo 67.
7. Qtd. in Griswold del Castillo 64.
8. Qtd. in Susan Ferriss and Ricardo Sandoval, *The Fight in the Fields: Cesar Chavez and the Farmworkers Movement* (New York: Harcourt Brace & Co., 1997) 61.
9. Huerta 216.
10. Huerta 216.
11. Huerta 216.
12. Huerta 216.
13. Huerta 216-217.
14. Qtd. in Griswold del Castillo 66.

15. Jean Murphy, "Unsung Heroine of La Causa," *Regeneración* Vol. 1, no. 11, 1971.
16. Barbara Baer, "Stopping Traffic: One Woman's Cause," *The Progressive* Sept. 1975.
17. "Dolores Huerta Talks About Republicans, Cesar, Children, and Her Home Town," *Regeneración* Vol. 2, no. 4, 1975.
18. Qtd. in Griswold del Castillo 67.
19. Qtd. in Jaques E. Levy, *Cesar Chavez: Autobiography of La Causa* (New York: W. W. Norton & Co., Inc., 1975) 126.
20. Qtd. in Levy 127.
21. Qtd. in Ferriss 76.
22. Qtd. in Ferriss 77.
23. Qtd. in Ferriss 77.
24. Qtd. in Ferriss 77.
25. Luis Valdez, "Dolores Huerta: A Tribute," *San Francisco Examiner Sunday Image Magazine* 12 Aug. 1990, qtd. in Griswold del Castillo 70.
26. Qtd. in Griswold del Castillo 71.
27. Baer 40.
28. Levy 262.
29. Ronald B. Taylor, *Chavez and The Farm Workers* (Boston: Beacon Press, 1975) 229-230.
30. Julie Felner, "Woman of the Year for Lifetime of Championing Rights of Farmworkers," *MS Magazine* Vol. 8, no. 4, Jan. 1998: 48.
31. Qtd. in Rose 437.
32. Felner 48.
33. Felner 48.
34. Qtd. in Felner 49.
35. Qtd. in Rose 434.

Recommended Reading

BOOKS

Arnesen, Eric, ed. *The Human Tradition in American Labor History*. Wilmington, DE: S R Bks., 2004.

Chavez, Cesar. *The Words of César Chávez*. Ed. by Richard J. Jensen and John C. Hammerback. College Station, TX: Tex. A&M Univ. Pr., 2002.

Dubofsky, Melvyn, and Van Tine, Warren, eds. *Labor Leaders in America*. Urbana, IL: Univ. of Ill. Pr., 1987.

Dulles, Foster R., and Dubofsky, Melvyn. *Labor in America: A History*. 7th ed. Wheeling, IL: Harlan Davidson, 2004.

Ferriss, Susan, and Sandoval, Ricardo. *The Fight in the Fields: Cesar Chavez and the Farmworkers Movement*. New York: Harcourt, 1997.

Griswold del Castillo, Richard. *César Chávez: A Triumph of Spirit*. Norman, OK: Univ. of Okla. Pr., 1995.

Hammerback, John C., and Jensen, Richard J. *The Rhetorical Career of César Chávez*. College Station, TX: Tex. A&M Univ. Pr., 1998.

Huerta, Dolores Fernandez. "Un Soldado del Movimiento" *With These Hands: Working Women on the Land*, by Joan M. Jensen. Old Westbury, NY: Feminist Pr., 1981. Huerta's essay is in English.

La Botz, Dan. *César Chávez and La Causa*. New York: Pearson Longman, 2006.

Levy, Jacques. *Cesar Chavez: Autobiography of La Causa*. New York: Norton, 1975.

McGregor, Ann, and Wathen, Cindy, eds. *Remembering Cesar: The Legacy of Cesar Chavez*. Clovis, CA: Quill Driver Bks., 2000.

Phelan, Craig. *Grand Master Workman: Terence Powderly and the Knights of Labor*. Westport, CT: Greenwood, 2000.

Powderly, Terence V. *The Path I Trod*. Ed. by Harry J. Carman, Henry David, and Paul N. Guthrie. New York: Columbia Univ. Pr., 1940.

Rose, Margaret. "Dolores Huerta" *Dictionary of Hispanic Biography*. Detroit, MI: Gale Research, 1996.

Streissguth, Thomas. *Legendary Labor Leaders*. Minneapolis, MN: Oliver Pr., 1998.

Weir, Robert E. *Beyond Labor's Veil: The Culture of the Knights of Labor*. University Park, PA: Penn. State Univ. Pr., 1996.

WEB SITES

American Federation of Labor-Congress of Industrial Organizations <http://aflcio.org>

Dolores Huerta Foundation <http://www.doloreshuerta.org>

Feminist Majority Foundation <http://www.feminist.org>

United Farm Workers of America. <http://www.ufw.org>

Glossary

Abolitionist *(AB uh LIHSH uh nihst)* a person who favored the end of slavery in the United States in the 1700's and 1800's.

anarchist *(AN uhr kihst)* a person who wants to overthrow governments and have a world without rulers and laws.

assembly line a row of workers and machines along which work is passed until the final product is made.

barrio *(BAHR ree oh)* Spanish word for neighborhood.

bracero *(bruh SAIR oh)* a Mexican laborer who enters the United States under contract on a legal, temporary basis to work for a specified employer.

boycott to join together and have nothing to do with a person, business, nation, employer, or any other person or thing in order to coerce or punish.

campesino *(KAHM pay SEE noh)* Spanish word for an agricultural worker.

Chicano *(chee KAH noh)* any person living in the United States who was born in Mexico or is descended from people born in Mexico.

company town a town built by or around, and owned and operated by, a large corporation.

cooperative an organization in which profits and losses are shared by all members.

DDT dichloro-diphenyl-trichloroethane, an insecticide that has been widely used on crops for pest control.

Dust Bowl a series of destructive wind and dust storms that struck the United States during the 1930's.

factory farm the large-scale, industrialized rearing of livestock by a large agricultural corporation.

Gilded Age a period of economic growth—with social problems beneath the surface—that lasted roughly from the end of the American Civil War (1860–1865) until 1900.

Grand Master the head of an order of knighthood, a lodge, or a council.

Great Depression a worldwide business slump in the 1930's, ranking as the worst period of high unemployment and low business activity in modern times.

hacienda *(HAH see EHN duh)* a large farm or country estate in Spanish America.

Hispanic a person living in the United States who is of Spanish or Latin American descent.

labor union a group of workers joined together to protect and promote their interests.

migrant worker a person who travels from one area to another in search of work.

pachuco *(puh CHOO koh)* Spanish slang referring to a Mexican American teen-ager who dresses in flashy clothes.

picket line a group of persons at or near a factory, store, or other establishment trying to prevent employees from working or customers from buying.

proletarian the lowest class in economic and social status.

scab a workman who will not join a labor union or who takes a striker's place.

segregation the separation of one racial group from another or from the rest of society, especially in schools, restaurants, and other public places.

sharecropper a person who farms land for the owner in return for part of the crops.

strike the act of stopping work in order to get better pay or shorter hours, or to force an employer to meet some other demand.

suffragette a woman supporter of the right of women to vote.

tenant farmer a farmer who raises crops or livestock on land that belongs to another person, to whom the tenant pays rent in cash or in a share of the crops or livestock.

Index

Page numbers in *italic* type refer
to pictures.